WAKING THEIR NEIGHBORS UP

WAKING THEIR NEIGHBORS UP

The Nashville Agrarians Rediscovered

THOMAS DANIEL YOUNG

*MERCER UNIVERSITY
LAMAR MEMORIAL LECTURES
No. 24*

THE UNIVERSITY OF GEORGIA PRESS

ATHENS

975.
I29xy

Copyright © 1982 by the University of Georgia Press
Athens, Georgia 30602

All rights reserved

Set in 11 on 13 pt. Baskerville
Printed in the United States of America

Library of Congress Cataloging in Publication Data

Young, Thomas Daniel, 1919–
Waking their neighbors up.

(Lamar memorial lectures; no. 24)
Bibliography: p.
Includes index.
1. American literature—Southern States—History and criticism. 2. Authors, American—Southern States—Political and social views. 3. Literature and society—Southern States. 4. Southern States—Civilization. 5. Nashville (Tenn.)—Intellectual life.
6. American literature—20th century—History and criticism. I. Title. II. Series.
PS261.Y63   810'.9'975   81-14736
ISBN 0-8203-0600-2   AACR2

83-3220

For Tom and Kathy

Contents

Foreword

THE YEAR 1980 MARKED THE FIFTIETH ANNIVERSARY OF the publication of a remarkable volume entitled *I'll Take My Stand: The South and the Agrarian Tradition*. Believing that event to be worthy of commemoration and knowing that two contributors to the volume later had close ties with the Lamar Lectures—John Donald Wade as one of the organizers of the series and Donald Davidson as the first lecturer—Mercer University's Lamar Memorial Lectures Committee invited as the twenty-fourth lecturer an eminent authority on the Nashville Agrarians, Professor Thomas Daniel Young of Vanderbilt University.

Despite competition from presidential candidates debating on television the evening of the final lecture, all of Professor Young's lectures were well attended and well received. With his keen wit and easy manner, Mr. Young entertained his audiences. With his broad knowledge and deep understanding of the Agrarians, he informed us. In his lectures he traced the evolution of *I'll Take My Stand*, described its reception upon publication, accounted for the Agrarians' use of the rhetorical mode, and maintained that time has proved those essayists to be prophets.

Stung by attacks upon the South after the Scopes trial, the poets who comprised the Fugitive group at Vanderbilt—notably John Crowe Ransom, Donald Davidson, Allen Tate, and Robert Penn Warren—conceived the

idea of a symposium that would argue for the worth of
an ordered, traditional society such as that of the South
as an alternative to the misdirected, progressive society
that they perceived the North to be. As Mr. Young
noted, those poets and the eight other writers who contributed to *I'll Take My Stand* tried, like the New En-
glander Henry Thoreau nearly a hundred years before,
to "wake their neighbors up" to the perils of material
progress.

Many of their neighbors resented the alarm, and
some ridiculed it. In a response typical of urban newspapers, the Macon *Telegraph* described *I'll Take My Stand*
as the "high spot in the year's hilarity." More often the
volume was simply ignored, and it was out of print for
many years. At long last it was reissued in 1962 and
again in 1977. Today, in an age painfully sensitive to the
problems of mass society, the Agrarians' commentary on
the nature of man and their vision of the good life have
a special pertinence.

To enhance an awareness and appreciation of Southern culture was an abiding concern of Mrs. Eugenia
Dorothy Blount Lamar. To that end she established
these lectures through her will. Professor Young has
continued the tradition of excellent scholarship evident
in the series. For doing that, the Lamar Memorial Lectures Committee thanks him.

Wayne Mixon
for the
Lamar Memorial Lectures Committee

Preface

THE FIRST THREE CHAPTERS OF THIS BOOK ARE SLIGHTLY
revised and expanded versions of lectures delivered at
Mercer University on October 27 and 28, 1980. Chapter
Four sketches briefly the literary careers of the major
contributors to *I'll Take My Stand*, especially during the
years leading up to the publication of the second Agrarian symposium, *Who Owns America?* (1936). The final
few paragraphs of that chapter follow some of the
Agrarians as they initiate their next communal activity,
now commonly known as the New Criticism.

Any reader of this book can easily detect, I suspect,
evidences of my conviction that the basic attitudes that
inspired the writing of the essays in *I'll Take My Stand*
have had a profound influence upon Southern thought.
It appears certain now that the doctrines espoused by
the Southern Agrarians have moved beyond the Mason-
Dixon line.

Fifty years ago the Agrarians were regarded by many
as reactionary idealists, a group of professors, poets,
and novelists far removed from the mainstream of
American political and social thought. Today, however,
almost no one insists that a loss of touch with reality resulted in their attempting to impose upon an unsuspect-
ing public a naive kind of utopian conservation. Instead,
many applaud their attempts to warn us of the evils inherent in a social order dominated by uncontrolled material acquisitiveness.

I want to thank Professor Henry Y. Warnock and the other members of the Lamar Memorial Lectures Committee for inviting me to give the twenty-fourth set of lectures in this distinguished series. My wife, Arlease, and I are especially grateful to Pat and Henry Warnock for their gracious hospitality and for the care with which they introduced us to their charming and beautiful city. We would also like to express our gratitude to President R. Kirby Godsey and the other members of the Mercer University faculty and staff and to John Eidson for their considerate and flattering attention and for their many efforts to make us feel welcome.

My most sincere appreciation goes to Charles East of the University of Georgia Press for his efforts to convert a series of lectures directed to a listening audience into a manuscript intended for readers. I am deeply indebted to Louis D. Rubin, Jr., and Virginia Rock, as the essays that follow amply demonstrate. Finally I should like to thank Frederick L. Hull and Thomas D. Young, Jr., for their invaluable assistance in preparing the manuscript and Louise Durham and Jewell Cooper for typing it in its several drafts.

THOMAS DANIEL YOUNG

Vanderbilt University
February 1981

WAKING THEIR NEIGHBORS UP

ONE

Evolution and Reception

THE FIRST ISSUE OF THE *FUGITIVE*, WHICH APPEARED IN Nashville in April 1922, contained thirty pages of original verse written by John Crowe Ransom, Donald Davidson, Allen Tate, Alec B. Stevenson, Stanley Johnson, Walter Clyde Curry, and Sidney Mttron Hirsch. This little magazine, destined to become an important force in twentieth-century poetry, also carried a brief foreword, written by Ransom, which announced rather majestically that one hope of the contributors was to open the channel so that Southern literature, which had expired "like any other stream whose source is stopped up," might flow again. To accomplish their objective these young poets felt they must flee "from nothing faster than from the high-caste Brahmins of the Old South." The first issue opened with "Ego," a poem by Ransom that suggests something of the feeling of separation from society which the group felt. One stanza of that poem reads as follows:

> So I take not the vomit where they do,
> Comporting downwards to the general breed;
> I have run further, matching your heat and speed,
> And tracked the Wary Fugitive with you.[1]

There is little doubt that these poets, like those the world over, felt they were isolated from the rest of society.

Although the *Fugitive* first published most of Ransom's mature poetry and some of his first important critical essays, as well as much of the early verse of Davidson, Tate, and Robert Penn Warren, who joined the group in February 1924, there was little social criticism either in the poetry or in the brief essays it contained. Even "Antique Harvesters," which Ransom called his "Southern poem," first appeared in another journal.[2] When the *Fugitive* suspended publication in December 1925 after nineteen issues, Ransom assured its readers that the financial position of the magazine was sound and that "from the literary standpoint" there was no indication of any "stoppage in the quantity or the quality of Fugitive output."[3]

Since there was no unusual financial pressure and since there were no apparent signs that the literary stream was "stopped up," to repeat the figure of speech Ransom had used in the first issue, there has been considerable speculation on why the *Fugitive* ceased publication. As we look back upon the event with the advantage of more than fifty years of hindsight, the reason seems very clear. The members of the group who served as its nucleus—Ransom, Tate, Davidson, and Warren—had reached the point in their literary careers where they no longer felt the need of the *Fugitive*. Ransom's primary concerns were turning from poetry back to theoretical literary criticism, which for ten years or so before the *Fugitive* first appeared had been his primary interest, and he would spend the next two years composing a book of criticism that he later destroyed when it was rejected by a publisher.[4] Tate was looking for a wider audience for his verse and criticism and for a better literary climate in which he could practice his craft. He was determined to go to New York City to see if he could make his way as a professional man of letters.[5] Davidson was interested in writing a kind of poetry unsuited for the pages of a small journal; his mind was filled with the philosophical-narrative poems that became *The Tall Men*, poems much too long to be published in the *Fugitive*.[6] Warren had completed the requirements for his undergraduate degree at Vanderbilt and had moved on to complete his formal education at California, Yale, and Oxford.[7]

In his announcement that the *Fugitive* would discontinue publication, Ransom assured his readers that the members of the group would meet as usual, and they did, although far less regularly than they had for the past four years. At these meetings many projects were discussed, including the formation of a Fugitive press and the publication of an annual volume of Fugitive verse or an anthology of the best verse written by the Fugitive poets during and after the publication of the magazine. This discussion resulted in the appearance of *Fugitives: An Anthology of Verse* (1928). Between 1925 and 1928, however, other events occurred that altered the views of some of the Fugitives and caused them for a time to shift a major portion of their creative energies from poetry and literary criticism to political, social, and cultural criticism. The most important of these events, Donald Davidson writes in *Southern Writers in the Modern World*, the first of the Lamar Lectures, was the Dayton, Tennessee, trial of John T. Scopes, a high school science teacher, for teaching evolution:

I can hardly speak for others, but for John Ransom and myself, surely, the Dayton episode dramatized, more ominously than any other event easily could, how difficult it was to be a Southerner in the twentieth century, and how much more difficult to be a Southerner and also a writer. It was horrifying to see the cause of liberal education argued in a Tennessee court by a famous agnostic lawyer from

Illinois named Clarence Darrow. It was still more horrifying—and frightening—to realize that the South was being exposed to large-scale public detraction and did not know or much care how to answer.[8]

The response of both Ransom and Davidson was immediate. Ransom shocked some of his colleagues, including his chairman, Professor Edwin Mims, by defending religious fundamentalism vehemently and openly. Many of his father's fellow ministers in the Methodist church were appalled by some of the arguments that appeared in *God Without Thunder: An Unorthodox Defense of Orthodoxy*, which Ransom began to work on immediately but which was not published until 1930.[9] (Although the ministers generally agreed with Ransom's insistence on the need for an inscrutable God, one who cannot be comprehended by reason or explained by scientific fact, they were stunned when he called Christ a demigod who, against his will, was made a part of the Godhead by his disciples and by Saint Paul.)

Davidson at once began his defense of the South, a subject that would command a major portion of his creative energies for the remainder of his life. On May 15, 1926, he published in the *Saturday Review of Literature* an essay entitled "The Artist as Southerner" in which he pointed out the difficulties confronting the Southern artist who attempts to employ native materials. He urged his fellow artists to be forever conscious of their regional heritage; then he moved to an explicit statement of the basic theme of the essay: "Fundamentalism, in one aspect, is blind and belligerent ignorance; in another, it represents a fierce clinging to poetic supernaturalism against the encroachments of cold logic; it stands for moral seriousness."[10] This latter point Ransom makes with great force and conviction in *God With-*

out Thunder. In another essay published a little later in *Forum*, Davidson reacted more forcefully to the ridicule Northern journalists were piling upon the South because of the Dayton trial.[11] Although Davidson admitted that the South was making progress, sometimes against its will, he urged his fellow Southerners to move cautiously and deliberately so that they would not discover sometime in the future that that which they had adopted because it was new was vastly inferior to that which the new had replaced. Like the artist who is his subject in "A Mirror for Artists," Davidson was beginning his withdrawal "within the body of the [Southern] tradition" to a point from which he could perform his artistic functions with full confidence and "the greatest consciousness of his dignity as artist."[12]

In the meantime, from his position in New York, Allen Tate had written Ransom that "we must do something about Southern history and culture of the South."[13] Ransom wrote Tate—apparently on the same day—that he too was concerned that the needless attacks on the South by members of the Northern press were going unanswered. Tate suggested a "Southern symposium of prose" to both Ransom and Davidson, who discussed the proposal, and Davidson responded enthusiastically to Tate on March 21, 1927, that he would join the project and "go the limit." Formal planning for the symposium was definitely underway.[14]

During 1927 Davidson and Ransom—often joined by John Donald Wade, also from the English department at Vanderbilt, Frank Lawrence Owsley from the history department, and Lyle Lanier from the psychology department—held lengthy discussions of the proposed project. On many occasions Andrew Lytle, a 1925 graduate of Vanderbilt who had returned from his study of drama at Yale to settle near Nashville, came to the city to assure the group of his complete devotion to the principles that were emerging from the discussions. Ransom and Davidson were keeping Tate fully abreast of the developments in Nashville. On June 25, 1927, Ransom wrote Tate:

> About our joint Southernism: two considerations occur to me as bearing on the hopefulness of the cause: one is yourself, and many other men who exhibit the same stubbornness of temperament and habit; men of my acquaintance born and bred in the South who go North and cannot bring themselves to surrender to an alien mode of life; this fact, many times repeated within my own knowledge, argues something ineradicable in Southern culture. The other one: Croce (with one or two others) appears to have inspired a genuine and powerful revival of Italianism (in a most advanced aesthetic sense) among the younger generation of Italians. Why can't we? Look at the Vanderbilt crowd; the candidates are always there, just waiting to be shown what their cause is.[15]

No longer, obviously, did Ransom feel the need to flee from the "high-caste Brahmins of the Old South."

As usual Davidson's responses were less philosophical, less rational, and more personal and emotionally charged. "When I see that so-called magazine, The New South, . . . I get sick with the black vomit and malignant agues," he wrote Tate on May 9, 1927; "when I read Bruce Bliven in the New Republic, I am willing to take to my bed and turn up my heels,—except that I am too mad to die just yet, and itchin for a fight, if I could only find some way to fight effectively. If genuine sectional feeling could be aroused there might be some hope; I do not yet venture to say whether that is possible. John Ransom and I are greatly riled. . . . Let us keep thinking about this."[16] Almost two years later, on February 5, 1929, filled no doubt with the reactions to the conversations that were occurring in Calhoun Hall on the Vanderbilt campus, he wrote Tate:

My impression is that the people who are of your opinion and mine and John's about things Southern are few and far between, and furthermore of little influence. If there were a Southern magazine, intelligently conducted and aimed specifically, under the doctrine of provincialism, at renewing a certain sort of sectional consciousness and drawing separate groups of Southern thought together, something might be done to save the South from civilization. . . . Economics, government, politics, machinery—all such forces are against us. With the issue of prosperity before everybody's eyes, Southerners get excited about nothing else—except religion. . . . Where can we join up, with our mysterious doctrine of provincialism? Still, I believe in agitating. The losing cause is not always the better one, but it is in this case.

Ransom, Wade, and I have been trying to get up a symposium on Southern matters, but without success so far. Of the persons we approached, only one, Gerald Johnson, answered, and his answer showed that he didn't understand what we were talking about.[17]

Davidson concluded by reminding Tate that he was on their list of prospective contributors to the symposium and asking if he would write an essay.

In early 1929 Lytle wrote Tate that as soon as Tate's biography of Jefferson Davis was completed he should join the group in Nashville in a concerted effort to get the symposium in print, devoting, if necessary, "three to five years to a lucid and forceful restatement of our philosophy, for when the industrial powers dictate, there will never be the chance."[18] In an attempt to stir up some enthusiasm for the project, Ransom published two essays, "The South Defends Its Heritage" and "The South—Old or New?"[19] Both of these present in an emphatic manner some of the fundamental issues that would be argued in the proposed symposium. They both restate and emphasize a point Ransom had made to Tate in the fall of 1927: "Our cause is, we have sensed this at the same moment, the Old South. Lytle wrote me the other day from Yale, for instance, on the poor quality of the men up there. . . . I walk a great deal and throw fits over the physical beauty of this place. Our fight is for survival; and it's got to be waged, not so much against the Yankees as against the exponents of the New South."[20]

On July 29, 1929, Davidson wrote Tate:

> I hope very much that you will soon complete your labors and return to the States. . . . [Your] services are badly needed in a big fight which I foresee in the immediate future.
>
> It is this. For several months, with the partial and somewhat hesitating encouragement of Ransom, I have been agitating the project of a collection of views on the South, not a general symposium, but a group of openly partisan documents, centralizing closely around the ideas that you, Ransom, & I all seem to have in common. It would deal with phases of the situation such as the Southern tradition, politics, religion, art, etc., but always with a strong bias toward the self-determinative principle. It would be written by native Southerners of our mind—a small, coherent, highly selected group, and would be intended to come upon the scene with as much vigor as is possible.[21]

Although one who has read Ransom's letters and essays written in the late twenties may be astounded at Davidson's suggestion that the project commanded less than Ransom's complete sympathy, this letter does contain the earliest explanation of the specific form the group in Nashville wished the symposium to take. Tate responded to Davidson's letter, advising him that he had kept Warren, who was at Oxford at the time, completely informed of the plans for the symposium, that Warren concurred with the aims and purposes of the project and that he would contribute an essay.[22] Tate also proposed the formation of a "society, or an academy of Southern *positive* reactionaries," composed of fifteen active members, the framing of a "philosophical constitution," and the acquisition of a newspaper and a journal to "argue our principles." He concluded his letter with a list of topics that should be discussed in the symposium and the names of some prospective contributors outside the Nashville group, including Stark Young and John Gould Fletcher, who would contribute essays to the symposium.[23]

This exchange of letters between Davidson and Tate moved the project into a new phase. Instead of a vague notion of wanting to do something to counteract the bad publicity the South was getting from the Northern press, what they now had in mind was a defense of their sectional heritage, which only a few years before they were either oblivious to or felt a compelling urge to escape. They now had a concrete proposal: an admittedly partisan book, written by a few carefully chosen contributors on selected topics. The procedure for the writing and publication of this book of essays did not follow any preconceived, carefully thought-through plan. In the first place many of the suggested contributors either were not interested in the proposal or were actively opposed to it—among others, U. B. Phillips, William Yandell Elliott, Howard Mumford Jones, Gerald Johnson, and Stringfellow Barr. Fewer than half of the topics for essays initially suggested were covered in the published book.

If one were trying to assure the failure of a project, one could hardly improve on the procedure followed in putting together *I'll Take My Stand.* Everything about arranging for the publication of the symposium, it would seem, was wrong. First of all the contributors were scattered over two continents, from Nashville to New York, London, Oxford, and Paris. Many of them had never met, and some of them never would. No one was assigned or assumed editorial responsibilities, though Davidson did handle some of the minor editorial duties. To guarantee that there was little or no unity in the collection, that there was nothing to tie the individual essays together, almost nothing could be more effective than completing the introductory "Statement of Principles" after more than half of the essays had been written. To make certain that the quality of the writing in the book was uneven, one could hardly do better than the makers of *I'll Take My Stand* did: that is, choose contributors from as many disciplines as possible. It would help to assure that the essays in the collection covered the spectrum from the very good to the barely passable if the contributors included at one extreme a small group of men with established literary reputations— Ransom (three books of poetry and *God Without Thunder*), Stark Young (associate editor of *Theatre Arts Monthly*, drama critic for the New York *Times,* novelist), John Gould Fletcher (nine books of poetry, a study of folk history, a book on the film), Tate (a book of poetry and two biographies) and moved through such gifted and soon-to-be-influential writers as Robert Penn Warren and Andrew Lytle, whose careers were just getting started, to end with the inclusion of a graduate student who was publishing his first essay.

The compilers of the essays in *I'll Take My Stand* violated virtually every rule of publishing, yet they managed to get together a book that has proved to be almost unique in the twentieth century in its effective emphasis on the specific dangers of material acquisitiveness. In the process of finding contributors and choosing essay subjects, in preparing an introduction, in selecting a title, and in obtaining a publisher, they continued barely to avoid disaster.

By the end of 1929 a great deal had been done, but there was much work yet to do and many important decisions to make, and the tentative publication date was less than nine months away. The list of contributors was almost set: Ransom, Davidson, Lytle, Frank Lawrence

Owsley, and John Donald Wade had agreed to write essays on specific topics. Some of the essays were already underway, and general areas to be covered in the others had been agreed upon. H. C. Nixon, Stark Young, John Gould Fletcher, Lyle H. Lanier, and Henry Blue Kline had either agreed to write essays within a broadly defined area or were being given careful consideration as possible contributors. Because no one had been appointed to serve as editor, two matters that should have been handled routinely presented immediate problems. First, the introduction or credo, which should have been written at an early stage in the preparation of the book to serve as a focal point for the writers of the individual essays, was not forthcoming because no one had been assigned the specific responsibility of composing such a document. Finally Davidson, Lytle, and Ransom agreed to revise a statement written earlier by Ransom and tentatively called "Articles of an Agrarian Reform." Ransom was much displeased with this document, he wrote Tate, because it "illustrates my tendency to be formal, philosophic, and abstract in such writing."[24] Kline had read the statement and found it, he told Davidson, "too religious or revolutionary."[25] Ransom also thought it "too bulky and too difficult, . . . too various in its topics . . . too dogmatic, and not sufficiently tentative . . . too harsh and personal in its tone." If one reads this document, the reasons Ransom and Kline found it unsatisfactory are glaringly apparent. The opening general statement begins:

> The separate studies in this book were written without much collaboration. Nevertheless, there lay behind them a great deal of discussion among the writers, both in conversation and through correspondence. In the course of discussion there gradually developed a fairly close agreement upon certain economic principles. It was even thought that it might be of interest for the reader to know

to what extent the writers formed a single group, and might care to commit their joint faith to a written statement.

The individual articles are no more specific or concrete, and are even less indicative of the purpose of the essays to follow:

Article 1
The good life must be lived much closer to the land than the ruling American ideal permits. . . .

Article 2
Opposed to the Southern way of life is the orthodox American way which may be defined as the industrial way.

Article 3
. . . the South, even if poverty stricken, offers the most substantial exhibit of the good life to be found in this country. . . .

Article 4
We are preoccupied with the Southern life only in the degree that tactics make the South the immediate battleground. . . .

Article 5
The ruling American ideal is ordinarily defined in the phrase: Progress. . . . Industrial progressivists assume that it is our destiny to carry on endless hostilities against nature. . . .

Article 6
To this ideal we propose the ideal of a life which comes as soon as possible to terms with nature. . . .

Article 7
Among the occupations of leisure are two pointed ones: aesthetic enjoyment and religious contemplation. . . .

Ransom notes in subsequent Articles that the industrialists will admit "that certain economic evils follow in the wake of the machines"—for instance, overproduction, unemployment, and unequal distribution of wealth. The industrialists expect these evils to disappear, however, as soon as they develop bigger and better machines to increase production. What they appear unaware of—and this attitude worries the Agrarians—is the "spiritual poverty that marks the age of the machine." The remedy the Agrarians suggest is "simple but radical: The cancellation of the Ideal of Industrial Progress." [26]

Although Ransom, Davidson, and Lytle agreed to write separate drafts of a revised version of the Articles—the plan being to incorporate the best features of the separate versions into one that would be circulated among the contributors—only Ransom submitted a revised draft. This revision, which included some suggestions from Tate and Davidson, was not completed until the summer of 1930, after many of the individual essays had been completed, and was too late for separate publication, as the group had intended, in order to give advance publicity to the book. It is, however, in every way superior to its predecessor. It is more positive and concrete in statement, less didactic and dogmatic in tone. It functions well as a broad ideological umbrella under which most of the disparate views of the twelve contributors can find cover. More than any other essay in the book it provides a "concurrence of purpose and a continuity of thought." [27]

No one, the statement begins, proposes "an independent political destiny" for the South. The question to which the contributors to this symposium address themselves is "how far shall the South surrender its moral, social, and economic autonomy to the victorious principle of Union" (xxxviii)? [28] Younger Southerners must look critically at the advantages of becoming a New South that is only a replica of the typical industrial community. The present economic organization of the collective American society is industrialism, which means "the decision of society to invest its economic resources in the applied sciences" (xxxix). The uncritical application of these applied sciences—and the key word here is *uncritical*—"has enslaved our human energies to a degree

now clearly felt to be burdensome" (xxxix). The contribution that science could make to labor is to make it
easier and to give the worker economic security. It has
done neither. The work in a modern industrial plant is
likely to be boring and tedious; at the same time unemployment is increasing. The modern laborer's work "is
hard, its tempo is fierce, and his employment is inse-
cure. The first principle of a good labor is that it must be
effective, but the second principle is that it must be en-
joyed" (xl). Often under industrialism neither of these
occurs, and the modern emphasis on saving labor, forever asserting that "the saving of labor is pure gain," assumes that labor is an evil (xl).

There are other evils fostered by industrialism, as
even its advocates will admit, but they expect these
evils—overproduction, unemployment, and inequitable
distribution—to disappear as soon as bigger and better
machines are developed. Though more is produced and
more time is available for its consumption, "the tempo
of our labors communicates itself to our satisfactions,
and these also become brutal and hurried" (xlii). For all
these reasons, in addition to the fact that his desires are
often satiated and his life aimless, modern man has lost
his sense of vocation.

Under an industrial regime, furthermore, religious
views cannot expect to flourish.

Religion is our submission to the general intention of a nature that is
fairly inscrutable. . . . But nature industrialized, transformed into
cities and artificial habitations, manufactured into commodities, is
no longer nature but a highly simplified picture of nature. We receive the illusion of having power over nature, and lose the sense of
nature as something mysterious and contingent. The God of nature
under these conditions is merely an amiable expression, a super-
fluity, and the philosophical understanding ordinarily carried in the
religious experience is not there for us to have. (xlii)

As the religious experience is adversely affected under industrialism, so are the arts, which, like religion, depend on "a right attitude to nature." Not only religion and the arts, but the "amenities of life"—manners, hospitality, romantic love, "the social exchanges which reveal and develop sensibility in human affairs"—suffer under a strictly industrial system (xliii). These amenities are the means by which civilized man controls the imperfections in his nature and those in the social systems he effects. With their disappearance civilization is likely to fall.

Not only is the tempo of industrial life fast, Ransom's introduction continues, it is accelerating. In order to feed the incredible monster which man has created and to keep it strong, he must produce products for which he has neither need nor desire. To create false desires, and then to induce the consumer to gratify them, big business has produced high-powered advertising and personal salesmanship. As a consequence of these developments, men are prepared to sacrifice their "private dignity and happiness to an abstract social ideal, and without asking whether the social ideal produces the welfare of any individual man whatsoever" (vlvi). Opposed to the industrial society, on the other hand, is the agrarian society, one in which agriculture is the leading vocation, "a form of labor that is pursued with intelligence and leisure"(vlvii).

This statement, it seems to me, is much more direct and specific than its predecessor. It includes some sweeping indictments of twentieth-century society and serves as a credo to which the various contributors can react both intellectually and emotionally. What is amazing is that it seems to anticipate and prepare the reader for the arguments to come later in the individual essays.

In fact many of the essays were already finished, though Ransom had not seen nearly all of them before his "Introduction: A Statement of Principles" was written.

The lack of an editor presented another immediate problem, that of finding a publisher willing to bring out such a symposium in the financially troubled days of 1930. For several months Davidson had been corresponding with Lewis H. Titterton, an associate editor at Macmillan, about his personal publishing plans so he inquired about that firm's interest in bringing out "the Southern book." At about the same time Tate wrote to Eugene Saxton, an editor at Harper's, to see if he could arouse some interest there. Tate's activity was in response to a request from Ransom that he try to place "a symposium by eight or ten men, for fall publication if the manuscript must be submitted by April 30; or a symposium by 10 or 12 men if it may be submitted as of July 1 or 15."[29] During the early part of 1930, therefore, negotiations were carried on simultaneously with both firms, and both agreed to take the book at about the same time. On February 18, Tate sent a telegram from New York indicating Harper's had agreed to publish the book. Three days later Davidson received a contract from Macmillan. On February 22, Ransom wrote Tate of their sudden and unexpected abundance of riches but urged him not "to weaken on the Harper's proposition." Three days later he wrote Tate that the contributors in Nashville had met and authorized him to sign the contract offered by Harper's.[30]

With his feelings somewhat ruffled, Davidson insisted that someone be appointed editor "to act as a clearing house and prodder" so that there would be no more mix-ups like that of securing a publisher. By common consent it was agreed that he would receive and edit the incoming essays and call upon the others for any help he needed. Another crisis arose almost immediately. From Oxford, Robert Penn Warren sent his essay on the position of the Negro in the south, the most controversial subject covered in the book. After Davidson read the essay he was deeply disturbed. He thought it "too progressive" and was convinced, he told Ransom, that its central thesis was diametrically opposed to "our ideas as I understand them." He wrote Tate that the essay "doesn't sound like Red [Warren] at all," and he doubted that it should be included. Davidson particularly disagreed with Warren's referring to black actor Paul Robeson's wife as "Mrs. Robeson," and to his repeated insistence that Southern whites were reneging on their obligation to allow black citizens of the region to develop to the fullest extent of their capacity. Davidson showed the essay to Lyle Lanier, who seemed to share his misgivings, and to Ransom, whose feelings, Davidson wrote Tate, "were mixed." He sent the essay to Tate, who showed it to Lytle, and Tate assured Davidson that they agreed that the essay was excellent and should be accepted. It was, of course, but there are indications that it was somewhat revised before it appeared in *I'll Take My Stand* as "The Briar Patch."

With two-thirds of the essays in, the credo prepared, and the contract for publication signed, the book still had no title. After several prospective titles were mentioned by various members of the group, John Donald Wade one day suggested *I'll Take My Stand* and Davidson added a colon and *The South and the Agrarian Tradition*. After consulting Ransom, Owsley, and Lanier—none of whom raised any serious objections—Davidson considered the matter settled. Several weeks later, however, Warren wrote Tate: "I think the title . . . is the Goddamndest thing I ever heard of; for the love of God block it if you can."[31]

A little while later Lytle was visiting Tate at his farm near Clarksville and they discussed Warren's objections and agreed that the title was inappropriate. They asked Davidson to report their dissatisfaction with the proposed title to Ransom. Lytle said later he felt Davidson had not indicated the seriousness of their disagreement but had merely indicated that another title, *Tracts Against Communism*, had been suggested.[32] The choice of title was mentioned in many of the letters exchanged among members of the group during the summer of 1930. Nixon indicated that he thought the "suggested title appropriate." Kline had some misgivings but could not suggest one he considered better. In June Lytle wrote Tate that he should find out if the title could be changed. At about the same time Davidson wrote Tate: "So far as I am personally concerned, and I think Ransom feels the same way, I'd be quite content to have you title the book." But he repeated that Ransom, the other contributors in Nashville, and he all thought "the present title a pretty good one." In late July a representative from Harper's visited Nashville, indicated his firm's satisfaction with the title, and expressed his conviction that it must stand because the book had already been advertised as *I'll Take My Stand: The South and the Agrarian Tradition*. Davidson reported this discussion to Tate and indicated he thought it was too late to change the title. Tate was not appeased, however, and threatened to withdraw his essay. He finally consented to its inclusion if he were allowed to add a footnote indicating his objections to the title.[33]

Despite Tate's objections, which as it turned out were well founded, the title performed a definite function in that it served the immediate practical purpose of giving a semblance of unity to the widely varied approaches, conclusions, and techniques employed in the individual essays. The first reviews of the book, however, seemed to support Tate's fears, voiced in his footnote, that the title would not "adequately and truthfully" express the aims of the contributors. "I observe," he wrote Davidson shortly after the book's appearance, "that [one reviewer] today on the basis of the title defines our aims as an 'agrarian revival,' and reduces our real aims to nonsense." "My melancholy," he concluded, "is profound."[34] Even Davidson, after reading the early reviews, agreed that *I'll Take My Stand* was the "most misunderstood *unread* book in American literature."

As Louis D. Rubin, Jr., argues, however, the term "Agrarianism" served as a focal point for the individual essays, providing a loose kind of unity even before the "Statement of Principles" was completed and circulated. It allowed men of diverse beliefs and expectations to operate around a central point. It embraced Ransom's conviction that the culture of the Old South was a continuation of that of Western European civilization, that the dominant American way, with its emphasis on material acquisitiveness, was the deviation. It covered H. C. Nixon's argument that the economy of the Southern farmer had long been at the mercy of corporate finance and a federal government that obviously had attempted to protect and foster industrial development. It included both Frank Owsley's conviction that Southern sectionalism was rooted in the long-established differences between an industrial and an agrarian economy, and Donald Davidson's interest in regional loyalty and his distrust of a needlessly complicated urban, industrial, big-government economy. It provided room both for Lytle's plea for a retention of Southern folkways developed and maintained by the Southern yeoman farmer and for Stark Young's image of a paternalistic, aristocratic society that has retained some of what Ransom

d call its "aesthetic forms": the manners, customs,
...ny and community loyalties, rites, rituals, and ceremonies of a traditional society. Certainly it gave John
Donald Wade ample opportunity to develop the portrait
of a man who in his every thought and action exempli-
fied these virtues. As a matter of fact the term seems to have served
everyone well except Tate, who argued for the return
of religious humanism, and Warren, who was obviously
at a disadvantage attempting to convince his readers of
the advantages of an agrarian over an industrial society
for the economic and social advancement of the black
man and woman in the South. As Warren affirmed
some years later, in repudiating the separate-but-equal
argument of his essay, his real interest in the symposium
was his fear of what a materialistic, positivistic social
order was doing to the freedom and integrity of the
individual.[35]

In the years since *I'll Take My Stand* was published,
most of the significant commentators on Southern culture have demonstrated their awareness of its existence,
although it has not been universally praised. Recently it
was included among the twenty-five most influential
books published about Southern culture in the twentieth century. At the time of its appearance, however, although it was widely reviewed, many of the reviews
were far from complimentary. More often than not it
was grossly misunderstood.

In her unpublished dissertation "The Making and
Meaning of *I'll Take My Stand*," Virginia Rock lists more
than twenty-five Southern newspapers that carried no-
tices of the book's appearance and almost that many
from those in cities outside the region, including five
New York papers as well as some in St. Louis, Buffalo,
Detroit, Hartford, Boston, Chicago, Omaha, and Des

Moines. William S. Knickerbocker, editor of the *Sewanee Review*, wrote in the *Saturday Review of Literature* that it was "the most challenging book published in the United States since George's *Progress and Poverty*." John Temple Graves called it a good "antidote to the platitudes of progress." The reviewer in the Des Moines *Register* expressed the belief that the writers of *I'll Take My Stand* "are very likely to form a nucleus for hundreds of more writers, who will be encouraged by the call of these men." John Peale Bishop declared that he was in complete sympathy with the central thesis of the book, and T. S. Eliot, writing in the *Criterion*, decided that "it is a sound and right reaction which impelled Mr. Allen Tate and his eleven Southerners to write their book."

Much of the reaction, of course, was much less favorable. A columnist in the Macon *Telegraph* called the volume "a high spot in the year's hilarity." The Nashville *Tennessean* interviewed Chancellor James H. Kirkland of Vanderbilt, who was quoted as saying: "You can't get back to the agrarian scheme of things. There are arguments on both sides as to the virtues of each system of living, but it's an entirely academic discussion because the anti-industrial plan is impractical." (The Agrarians should have expected little sympathy from the good Chancellor—he had refused to pay a dollar a year to subscribe to the *Fugitive*.) Henry Hazlitt accused the Agrarians of attempting to stem "the tide of progress." H. L. Mencken attacked the book in both the *American Mercury* and the *Virginia Quarterly Review*, declaring that the farmers are "doomed to become proletarians and the sooner the change is effected the better."[36]

Although *I'll Take My Stand* was more often ridiculed than championed, those responsible for its publication must have received some satisfaction from the fact that it was not ignored. Because of the controversy aroused by the book, the Agrarians were able to present their cause directly to the people. Ransom debated Stringfellow Barr before 3,500 people in Richmond, William S. Knickerbocker before 1,000 in New Orleans (Davidson also faced Knickerbocker in Columbia, Tennessee); Barr and Ransom met again in Chattanooga, and Ransom debated William D. Anderson, president of the Bibb Manufacturing Company, before an Atlanta audience estimated to be in excess of 1,500.

Nothing he did in connection with Agrarianism, Ransom said later, gave him greater pleasure than these debates because they offered the opportunity to present Agrarian views before interested and enthusiastic, if not always sympathetic, audiences. If we look closely at the contents of the remarks offered by Ransom's and Davidson's opponents, we can readily perceive how badly the Agrarian views were misunderstood. Time after time the Agrarians were accused of attempting to offer an acceptable alternative to industrialism by reversing the clock. (On the wall of his study above his desk in Gambier, Ohio, where he lived after leaving Vanderbilt, Ransom had a clock with hands that moved backwards across its face. It was given to him, he once said, by some of his Northern friends who called it his "Southern clock.") But none of the Agrarians thought they could disrupt the orderly movement of time; instead they were protesting against certain trends in modern society: its material acquisitiveness, its spiritual disorder, its lack of purpose, its destruction of individual integrity.

TWO

The Rhetorical Mode

THE QUALITY OF THE WRITING IN *I'LL TAKE MY STAND* IS
very uneven. To make this statement is not to propose
the unexpected to anyone familiar with the background
and achievements of the twelve contributors at the time
the symposium was published. Among them were five
men of letters with established reputations and nearly
two dozen books to their credit. (In their careers they
would publish collectively more than a hundred.) The
contributors also included five others who had written at least one book. Among these was Robert Penn
Warren, at the outset of the brilliant career in which
he would become one of the most prolific of the group.
Another was Andrew Lytle, actor, playwright, and soon-
to-be biographer and novelist—a young man with an
enviable talent. Another, John Donald Wade, was a
scholar, biographer, and man of talent and taste. Henry
Blue Kline's essay was the first and only publication
of its kind of his career, which included periods of employment as an industrial economist and journalist. By
design, too, the list of contributors, though obviously
centered around the talents of three men—John Crowe
Ransom, Donald Davidson, and Allen Tate—included
as many different disciplines and approaches to the central problem as possible. In addition to the men of letters, there was a political scientist and economist, a psy-
chologist, a historian, a journalist.

Despite the evidence that would seem to dictate the contrary, *I'll Take My Stand* is singularly unified. Louis Rubin insists that the book is a permanent addition to the writings on American culture because of some of the basic points of agreement among its contributors, an underlying unity in their method of attack:

> It was a way of striking out against the deification of the machine, of warning against the depersonalizing forces of an unchecked, unrestrained industrial capitalism. It was not utopian so much as protest literature. The agrarian community which it imaged filled the function not of an economic alternative to the city, but of a pastorale rebuke giving warning of the fragmenting complexity of modern urban society. And like all pastorale, it was written not for shepherds but for city dwellers—for southerners who were already living in urban America.[1]

Although when it appeared *I'll Take My Stand* was "dismissed as being vague, sentimental, and impractical," as Cleanth Brooks has written, it is now understood to be a profound assessment of our civilization. On the other hand, many of the glittering promises of the future made under the assumption that they were practical and highly productive have proved invalid. For example, the energy shortage makes our sprawling suburbs, our interstates, suburban supermarkets, and enormous fleets of automobiles look suddenly unrealistic. What *I'll Take My Stand* offers, Brooks says, is "a base for the development of certain fundamental assumptions about the 'good life' and what it truly is and about the relations of means to ends in modern America." More than for the answers it proposes, *I'll Take My Stand* is important for the questions it asks.[2]

For these reasons and others that could be cited, and some that will be referred to later, it is evident that *I'll Take My Stand* is much more than a statement of short-term political policies and economic strategies. One way, I think, to understand more fully its durability, to perceive some of the reasons why after fifty years and more it is still being read—still continues to receive the attention of some of the most seriously engaged students of modern democracy when so many other books of its kind have long since gone out of print or are collecting dust on library shelves—is to examine carefully the individual essays, to discover if we can see exactly what argument each of the contributors is presenting and the rhetorical devices he employs in attempting to make his argument plausible.

The mode of discourse used in this book of essays is that which Allen Tate has described as the rhetorical, one that "presupposes somebody at the other end silently listening."[3] The speaker or writer involved in this mode is one of definite convictions derived from an absorbing contemplation of the concrete particularities of the world he inhabits; he harbors definite feelings toward that specific place. He is not anyone living anywhere; he is Donald Davidson of Chapel Hill, Tennessee, or Robert Penn Warren of Guthrie, Kentucky. His convictions, attitudes, and feelings of place—home, community, section—are so much a part of him that he feels a deep-seated compulsion to persuade his listener or reader to his point of view. A close look at some of the essays will reveal the broad variety of rhetorical devices and principles used by the individual essayists in an attempt to make their argument convincing. One reason for the durability of *I'll Take My Stand* is undoubtedly the skilled use of these devices by the writers of the separate essays.

The opening essay, "Reconstructed but Unregenerate" by John Crowe Ransom, really a composite of two previously published essays, is in a way a kind of keynote statement in that it suggests in broad terms many of the specific ideas presented in later essays.[4] Beginning with a leisurely description of a contemporary Southern society apparently so impotent and harmless that Northerners send their daughters but not their sons to school here, Ransom moves quickly to a presentation of two concepts around which his essay is organized—the Idea of Progress and the Idea of Service. Americans, he asserts, serve an Idea of Progress. They are not content to live in accord with nature; they must demonstrate their superiority over it. In such a society the loving arts, religions, and philosophies cannot exist because "Progress never defines its ultimate objective, but thrusts its victims at once into an infinite series" (8). Closely related to this concept, he argues, is that of Service, which is intended to demonstrate the dream of the American to overcome material opposition. Man's ambition causes him to rage relentless war against nature, never realizing that this is a battle he can never win. He deludes himself with ideas of false victories, but nature always reasserts its superiority. If he would forsake his attempts to harness nature so that he could garner a massive share of the world's goods, he could learn to respect nature, and from this respect he could receive that "primary joy, which is an inexhaustible source of arts and religions and philosophies" (9). Progress and Service, which manifest man's ambition to keep up materially with the most affluent members of his community, are predicated on man's increasing control over nature until finally at some unknown time in the future he will control it completely. Such a view, Ransom argues, brutalizes man because it allows "no deep sense of beauty, no heroism of conduct, and no sublimity of religion." Such feelings are bred "by the humble sense of man's precarious position in the universe" (10).

Ransom's intent in presenting these two metaphorical assertions—the Ideas of Progress and Service—is to suggest that the typical American attitude is to continue to pioneer long after the need to pioneer has passed, to do what he calls "pioneering on principle." The meaning he intends to convey by that term is suggested elsewhere in his essay "Forms and Citizens."[5] In its pioneering or formative stage, he writes in that essay, a society must concentrate upon its "economic forms," those of intense practicality, the "recipes of maximum efficiency, short routes to 'success,' to welfare, to the attainments of natural satisfactions and comforts."[6] The traditional forms of such objects as "plough, table, book, biscuit, machine, and of such processes as shepherding the flock, building, baking, making war" are absolutely essential to man's well-being when all of his energy must be expended in wresting a living from the soil, protecting himself from savage enemies, and trying to exist in an environment in which he is faced on every hand by unfriendly or uncooperative forces. When man continues to devote the major portion of his time and energy to such forms, when he acts as if the "whole duty of man" is to "increase material production" when that time is past, then man or his social order, Ransom says, is "pioneering on principle."

The South, unlike the North, pioneered its way to a sufficiently comfortable kind of establishment; then, believing man should relax and enjoy the fruits of his economic order, the South began to develop its aesthetic forms—rites, rituals, manners, customs, ceremonies, religion—and to perpetuate a civilized way of life. These "aesthetic forms," Ransom asserts, "are a technique of restraint, not of efficiency. They do not butter our bread, and they delay the eating of it. They stand between the individual and his natural object and impose a check upon his action."[7] It is only too easy to define industrialism, he says in his essay in *I'll Take My Stand*, because it is the modern form of pioneering, "a program under which men, using the latest scientific paraphernalia, sacrifice comfort, leisure, and the enjoyment of life to win Pyrrhic victories from nature at points of no strategic importance" (15).

Western European civilization is the result, however, of the development of these aesthetic forms. They teach us that we cannot handle our natural objects as quickly and as rudely as we please. The kind of process that I believe Ransom has in mind is the means by which human love is developed. The caveman took the object of his desire by the hair of the head, carried her to his cave, and there, by direct assault (the method of the economic forms), took what he wanted. In a civilized society, through aesthetic forms, the caveman's instinctive natural desire is developed into the higher, more complicated emotion of human love. First there is the debutante's ball or coming-out party at which the girl's parents declare she is physically ready to receive the attention of the opposite sex. This occasion is followed by a period of association between the young people of both sexes known as courtship to allow them to become better acquainted. After a time the number of suitors decreases until there is only one girl and one boy, and at the appropriate time an engagement is formally announced, followed by a series of parties and finally a public exchange of vows. What this lengthy, inexpedient, and economically useless process has accomplished is to breed, nurture, and bring to fruition the very involved emotional state that only civilized man can know. The feeling of lust which the caveman shared with all other animals has evolved into love. The caveman's desire for *any* woman has been converted, though it has lost none of its intensity, into desire for *one* woman, and thus the basis for monogamous marriage and the family unit, the foundation of any civilized society, has been formed.[8]

Just as man shifted his affection from all women to one woman and in the process formed a deep personal attachment that the caveman could not experience, so the small farmer living on the homestead occupied by his family for generations develops a relationship with that homestead which the traditionless city dweller cannot know. This, I believe, is what Ransom is in effect saying.

The farmer who is not a mere laborer, he writes in his essay in *I'll Take My Stand*,

> identifies himself with a spot of ground, and this ground carries a good deal of meaning; it defines itself for him as nature. He would till it not too hurriedly and not too mechanically to observe in it the contingency and the infinitude of nature; and so his life acquires its philosophical and even its cosmic consciousness. A man can contemplate and explore, respect and love, an object as substantial as a farm. . . . But he cannot contemplate nor explore, respect nor love, a mere turnover, such as an assemblage of "natural resources," a pile of money, a volume of produce, a market, or a credit system. (19)

Through the use of the twin metaphors of Progress and Service—by which he can contrast two views of the social order—Ransom places before the reader the basic philosophical difference between agrarianism and industrialism that many of the essays following his will comment on more specifically.

In "A Mirror for Artists" Donald Davidson develops his argument quite differently from the manner in which Ransom has presented his. First Davidson postulates a

conviction and then garners all the details that time and
space will permit as he attempts to convince his reader
of the validity of that position. In an industrial society,
he asserts, there will be no art of quality, for that which
does appear will be distorted and inferior. Since the industrial revolution, Davidson argues, the position of the
artist has been a special one. Rather than being a valued
member of society, he has been *against* or *away from* society and this separation becomes his essential theme.
He may retire within his tradition to a point at which he
can speak with conviction, "like a weaponless warrior
who plucks a sword from the tomb of an ancient hero"
(44). Or, more likely, he will sing to an ever diminishing
audience until he is singing only to his fellow artists, or,
finally perhaps, only to himself. In the process of losing
his position as a functioning member of society, the artist develops a personal style, usually obscure, and writes
on esoteric subjects.

Another reason an industrial society will distort the
arts it produces, Davidson says, is its basic misunder-
standing of the nature and function of art. Rather than
treating art as the result of a basic human need, it con-
siders the art product, in Ransom's term, as an economic
form, as a commodity. Five- and ten-cent store magnates
will buy "pictures" as an investment and remove them
from circulation in order to increase their monetary value. History demonstrates that art assumes its proper position and receives appropriate attention when it comes
out of a society that is mostly religious, stable, and agrarian, where men are never too far removed from nature
to forget that art's chief subject is nature.

Industrialists promise to make art products available
to the masses through better distribution, subsidized art
galleries and museums, and huge lending libraries.
Such proposals are a further indication of these people's

abysmal ignorance of the relationship that should exist between the art object and its consumer. They propose to create a vast audience for art by having a panel of experts choose what is best, and through a National Arts Council (or a National Endowment for the Arts) form a group of local committees to distribute the masterpieces chosen, or broadcast the world's best symphonies to millions. What these social planners do not realize is that a mechanized social order does not supply the kind of leisure we need for the appreciation of art. We live by the clock all of our waking hours—those allotted to work and those left for play are all devoted to feverish activity. Work and play are at cross purposes, and the human psyche cannot long withstand this pull from two different directions without suffering spiritual damage. Our work has become so monotonous that we demand that our leisure time be filled with pure entertainment. Any art that is produced and distributed for mass consumption is likely to be bad art. (A few hours before a TV set will certainly prove the validity of this statement. Most of the pap produced commercially is obviously designed to make one forget that tomorrow he must spend eight hours turning bolt 464 one-quarter round.)

Public education, which has come to be regarded as a panacea for all social ills, will not improve taste, for it must turn out vocational specialists. The more a student is impressed with the values of the humanities the more unhappy or ill-adjusted he will become in an industrial state.

We are confronted with a grave crisis, like that of war, Davidson continues, and the artist, even if he becomes less an artist, must step into the ranks to bear the brunt of the battle against the common foe. He must help to restore a social economy that is in danger of becoming hostile to his interests (51). Davidson's argument is supported by carefully chosen, salient details presented in lucid, concrete, convincing language.

Lyle Lanier employs yet another form of argumentation in his "A Critique of the Philosophy of Progress." His essay, which traces the idea of progress from its inception to the present, is a model of deductive reasoning. His reference is always to authority, from the ancient Greeks to John Dewey. If the doctrine of progress did not have such obvious and immense social significance in modern society, he begins, the only sensible view one could take of this philosophical concept would be to suggest that there is little agreement on its origin or its value. His present interest in tracing the development and analyzing the significance of the idea of progress, Lanier continues, is derived from his awareness that one modern thinker, Dewey, believes that industrial technology provides a means of securing progress and preserving our culture against decline, while another, Oswald Spengler, looks on industrialism and its concomitant manifestations as evidence of the decline of Western civilization. In an attempt to determine which of these views is the right one, Lanier first traces the development of the idea that man's journey through the world is progressive; then he attempts to explain why two of the most important philosophers of his day can disagree so completely on the nature of man's position in the modern world. What can reasonably be man's expectations for the future? Can he look forward with some confidence to the time when he will have corrected all social ills so that perfect men can live in a perfect society? Or will the social system progressively reflect the imperfections of its creators and constituents until this civilization will collapse like those that preceded it?

The doctrine of progress, Lanier attests, is really a modern idea. The concept of a chronological succession of events meant little to the ancient Greeks, who believed the human race was merely one episode in the history of the world. Time proceeded, they believed, according to a cyclical pattern which repeated itself forever (125). The principal problem of the Greek philosophers was that of attempting to find some kind of abiding essence in these eternal cycles. The Greek thinkers, therefore, had no philosophy of history, saw no human meaning in history as a continuum of time.

The Christians first introduced a sense of history into man's thought. Man was created free, but he committed sin; therefore his time on earth was merely an interlude between birth and death, a period in which through faith he could purge himself of sin and end his earthly existence by a return to heaven (126). With little interference from the Roman Empire, the church dominated man's thought for more than a thousand years. Under this system of thought, Lanier observes, there is obviously no prospect of man's progressing in this life. Man will labor always under the curse of the original sin, and his only hope of improving his lot is salvation and ascension to heaven when he dies. The only systematic thought of the period was Scholasticism, in which Aquinas and the Thomists attempted to rationalize Christian dogma.

Although Roger Bacon's interest in nature and natural science in the thirteenth century presaged the fall of Scholasticism, and the revival of letters in the fifteenth century accelerated the process, the church continued to dominate Western thought until the coming of a series of events in the sixteenth and seventeenth centuries (127). First Greek civilization was rediscovered, which, Lanier believes, when combined with the work of Copernicus, Kepler, and Galileo, inspired Renaissance thinkers to try to learn more about the natural world. The end result of these changes was the publication in the early seventeenth century of Francis Bacon's *The Advancement of Learning and Novum Organum* (128). These treatises set out to oppose Aristotelian logic, which sought to bring together a universal law (truth) and a particular fact of observation and to assert the validity of the individual in the light of this relationship. Bacon argued that knowledge can be discovered only by a careful study of the processes of nature. Such knowledge is important because it is the only means by which man can gain control over the world. The greater man's understanding of the way the world operates, Bacon reiterated, the better man's chances of controlling it for his benefit. With his work Bacon not only introduced inductive reason, but also paved the way for modern pragmatic thinking.

With the discovery of the sun as center of the universe and the development of the doctrine of Immanence, which postulated that God or an abstract mind is immanent in the universe, man's attention was directed from heaven to earth, and the age of modernism had its beginning. In the eighteenth century, then, all human institutions were subjected to rational analysis for the purpose of perfecting them if possible. From this kind of activity comes utilitarianism, which holds that an action is pleasing in proportion to the degree to which it aims at securing or secures the greatest happiness for the greatest number of people (129). The eighteenth century also produced Deism with its emphasis on an impersonal rather than a personal god (130).

This positivistic and rationalistic thought was opposed in the latter part of the eighteenth and the early part of the nineteenth centuries by a group of German thinkers. Kant rejected the doctrine of empirical knowledge and emphasized the organizing power of the mind. Hegel perceived reality as the evolution from primitive formless matter to the human organism, thus formulating the first complete doctrine of history showing a rational chronological development as improvement; that is, a doctrine of progress (130–31). Hegel's work cleared the way for the theories of scientific evolution of Lyell, Darwin, and Huxley, and, together with the work of Kant, initiated the doctrine of natural rights, which provided a concept of individualism permitting great personal autonomy and at the same time instituting social stability by insisting on man's attachment to land (133–35).

The industrial revolution resulted in a shifting population, the formation of urban centers, and the popularization of the doctrine of progress (134). Everyone was supposed to share in the material produce of an expanding industrial economy. That this course of events did not occur inspired Karl Marx to develop his theory of economic determinism, which seemed to guarantee the continual improvement of the worker and the social system under which he must live. The conquest of the West by machine technology produced social consequences unparalleled in history (135). William James postulated an indeterminate universe and introduced his theory of pragmatism, which strongly challenged the system of Christian ethics. John Dewey's instrumentalism insisted on the importance of all human institutions being involved in the achievement of moral values. The world is incomplete, he insisted, and can be improved by man's decisions and by the social, economic, and political institutions he develops. The idea of the world becoming better and better became a widely accepted philosophical position (136–51).

After this clear and lucid survey of a necessarily complex subject, and after carefully pausing to cite the authoritative explanation justifying man's changing views of the universe, Lanier finally arrives at the present. Although, as he pointed out in the beginning of his essay, there is no agreement among present-day philosophers about the doctrine of progress, Lanier's treatment of the thought of Dewey seems to make his position clear. Lanier does not believe that the world is becoming forever better and better, that as soon as social science can sufficiently improve the nature of man and the system in which he lives and as soon as science can solve the mysteries of the universe perfect men will live in a perfect world. Nor does he accept the notion that the millennium lies there in the foreseeable future and that man must eternally strive to bring it into being. Instead he seems to believe that any social, political, and economic system effected by man will reflect the imperfections of its creators; therefore he insists that since overproduction, unemployment, and inequitable distribution will always result under industrialism, the production of commodities should be carefully controlled and the large number of unemployed should be induced by every possible means to return to agriculture.

Allen Tate begins his "Remarks on the Southern Religion" by indicating that he is confronted with an impossible situation. He is expected to develop logical argument on a subject that does not lend itself to logical analysis. One can know metaphysical reality only through myth. Modern man's tendency to reduce to an abstract statement that which in reality he is unable to comprehend except through a mythical assertion has made a discussion of religion impossible. "For a myth,"

Tate argues, "should be in conviction immediate, direct, overwhelming, and I take it that the appreciation of this kind of imagery is an art lost to the modern mind" (156). Since he cannot present his subject through narrative or fable and since it will not permit logical development, he resorts to the use of analogy, to that which he will later call the "symbolic imagination," attempting to move from one step to another in his treatment through a ladder of analogies.[9] Man's overwhelming desire to reduce concrete reality into an abstract statement will not permit him to *know* God any more than he can fully perceive the horse grazing on his lawn. He cannot see the whole horse; he can only see the characteristics that this horse shares with all other horses, or the power of this horse that is known by the abstract term "horsepower." What the man of religious faith would know immediately is that the whole horse is there although he cannot see him; similarly, Tate adds, he would perceive the horse in its completeness although this essay cannot bring him forth. What modern man cannot believe is that there is more to the horse than the senses can perceive or the mind conceive. Modern man is unable to receive a vision of God because he has lost his power to transcend the boundaries of knowledge circumscribed by his senses and reason.

Having lost this power, and depending completely on his senses and reason, modern man can only see half a horse, that half that became a dynamo or an automobile. He knows the animal not in its wholeness—a concrete, particular horse different from any other horse that ever existed anywhere at any time—but he perceives only that part of the animal that can be converted into power. Because man can no longer reconstitute an image and an idea simultaneously, he has only a half-religion, a religion of how things work (157). The half-horse image becomes an emblem of modern man's religion because the part of the horse hidden from the man is irrational, an infinite object, unique and unpredictable.

How can man know that the religion of the utilitarian half of the horse is really a religion? It has no altars, no rituals, no ceremonies. These new "half-religionists," Tate insists, are simply worshipping a principle and ignoring what they do not wish to see. That which they do not wish to see is that a genuine religion, a religion of the whole horse, predicts *both* success and failure, as well as the traditional concepts of both good and evil (158). This kind of religion is what Ransom would call an economic, not an aesthetic, form, and is therefore bogus. It is practiced only because it is expedient and workable.

Tate then shifts his analogy, saying modern man's view of religion is similar to his view of history (160–63). There are two views of history. One is the *short view*—a concrete series that took place at a specific, definite time, a time full of senses and sensations, one replete with mysteries and uncertainties. Then there is the *long view*—a concept of history without images, only ideas, a set of principles, an abstraction which resists differentiation between the Roman and Greek civilizations. In the short view, history is the specific account of the doings of individualized men, who acted their roles in a vast setting "which somewhat bewildered them and which prompted them to make up stories with an obvious moral" (160–61). They were trying, as man always has, to explain the rationally inexplicable through myth.

The long view of history destroys tradition, Tate says. Just as man through it cannot differentiate between the Roman and Greek civilizations, he cannot perceive the distinction between the Christian myth and the myth of

Adonis. Since they are both vegetation rites, why prefer Christ over Adonis? The short view concentrates on the specific, the unique, the concrete, the particular, and through it one can detect the differences between Adonis and Christ, but too few modern men can employ the short view.

The difference between the Eastern and the Western mind is that the Eastern sensibility, unlike the Western, is not divided (163). The Western sensibility is split between "a self-destroying naturalism and practicality, on the one hand, and a self-destroying mysticism, on the other" (163). We cannot, in other words, let the entire horse fill our mind at once. We must forever attempt to defend the qualitative half of the horse against his abstraction, the practical half, and the only way we can mount a defense is through reason.

From his discussion of religion, which he thinks has disappeared because we have allowed the tradition that nurtured it to disintegrate through lack of use, Tate goes on to ask: How can tradition be defended? The answer, he says, is doubtless: "It can always be defended, but a recovery and restoration is a more difficult performance" (166). Although America has imitated the chief European economic and political forms, it has not retained the religious forms. The Old South was a feudal society without a feudal religion. The Jamestown project now impresses us as a "symbol of what later happened to this country: it was a capitalistic enterprise undertaken by Europeans who were already convinced adherents of large-scale exploitation of nature, not to support a stable religious order, but to advance the interests of trade as an end in itself" (166–67). The settlers of this colony represented a certain stage in the disintegration of religion, and their descendants have followed their leadership by becoming Protestant, ag-

gressive, and materially acquisitive. The religion that
has been dominant in the South (Tate apparently thinks
Catholicism would have been the appropriate one) is a
"non-agrarian and trading religion; hardly a religion at
all, but a result of secular ambition" (168). The reason
for the breakdown of the social structure after the Civil
War was the absence of a vital, all-enveloping religion.
Without an undergirding of this sort, the antebellum social system crumbled under the power of the onslaughts
to which it was subjected.

The antebellum Southern mind can be contrasted to
the New England mind of the same period, Tate says, by
examining the differences between the way Jefferson
and John Adams said they arrived at a decision. In a
moment of crisis Jefferson said he relied on taste, which
is a product of what Ransom calls the aesthetic forms,
"custom, breeding, ingrained moral decision." In a similar situation Adams said he always called upon a "process of moral reasoning" (170). At a moment of crisis,
then, Jefferson can react automatically, intuitively, but
Adams must ponder a decision by a process that is by
necessity based on abstract principles.

Although there is some evidence from this and other
examples which Tate gives elsewhere that the antebellum South had the instinctive basis for a proper religion, it was not organized around an appropriate my-
thology.[10] The rational life of its citizens was not united
with a religious experience. They had no rational defense, such as that which the Thomists gave to the medi-
eval Europeans, for the religious life. After the war,
then, like their Northern counterparts, they became ex-
ploiters of nature.

The modern Southerner, like the man at the ceme-
tery gate in Tate's "Ode to the Confederate Dead,"
might almost wish he could follow his Northern contem-

poraries and deny that history is made up of a vast body of concrete parts so that he too could fashion a religion out of abstractions. Had he not "Knowledge carried to the heart," he could wish that the ends of man could be reached by political means. If he had not once believed in the efficacy of the political system, so much of his energy would not have been devoted to politics, and the South might not have lost the Civil War.

Finally, Tate asks, how may the modern Southerner regain his tradition? By violence, he responds immediately, by an act of the conscious will. Since his religion was never sufficiently articulated and did not construct an appropriate myth, he can rely neither completely on faith nor on ritual and dogma. He must act on a decision rooted in reason and desire. He must genuinely want to become a part of his tradition, and he must make the decisions necessary to bring this about, willingly, decisively, and completely. He must cut away "the overgrowth" and get "back to the roots" (175). He "must use an instrument, which is political, and so unrealistic and pretentious that he cannot believe in it, to re-establish a private, self-contained, and essentially spiritual life. I say that he must do this; but that remains to be seen" (175).

Andrew Lytle's plea that the farmer avoid the temptations of finance capitalism and retain his independence through a retention or a restoration of subsistence farming presents even another form of argumentation. It is organized around the rhetorical principle of comparison and contrast. First Lytle portrays the life of the yeoman, subsistence farmer who continues to live on the place homesteaded by his ancestors, with his family

around him and his love of the land and his awesome
respect for a mysterious and contingent nature intact.
Lytle sketches the activities of a typical day.

On his two hundred acres, one hundred of which is in
cultivation, this yeoman farmer and his wife live in a
dog-run house with a brick walk running from the
porch to a horse block at the front gate. From there a
cedar-lined lane winds its way two hundred yards to the
main pike into Nashville. The house needs paint, but
the trees are whitewashed around the base of the trunk
for beauty and to protect them from the insects. The
central living place in the house, where the family
gathers, is the parents' bedroom, but the busiest spot is
the kitchen, where each meal is "a victory over nature, a
suitable union between the general principles of cook-
ery and the accident of preparation" (220). The fire in
the wood-burning stove must be kept at the right tem-
perature without a thermometer or the bread will not
rise; too much lard or too little will spoil the pastry; too
many or too few pinches of salt will spoil any dish. Cooking under these conditions is never boring, for it is an
art. The intention is always for perfection, and if it is to
be approached, if never attained, certain variable and
unexpected factors must always be controlled.

Activity begins in this house every morning at day-
light when the farmer gets out of bed and sounds the
rising bell—that is for everyone except the farmer's
wife, who has been in the kitchen for an hour making
preliminary preparations for cooking the morning
meal. At the sound of the bell the boys go to the barn to
feed the livestock, some of the girls go to the kitchen to
help their mother prepare breakfast, some feed the
chickens and others milk the cows, while the farmer
plans the activities of the day. Again, none of these activities is monotonous because, although basically the

same function is performed each day, there are always sufficient variables to make the work challenging.

After a breakfast of hot biscuits, eggs, ham, grits, molasses, jelly, and preserves—all homegrown or homemade—the men go to the fields and the women prepare the midday meal while one of the girls churns.

> This process takes a variable length of time. If the milk is kept a long time before it is poured up, the butter is long in coming. Sometimes witches get in the churn and throw a spell over it. In that case a nickel is dropped in to break the charm. The butter, when it does come, collects in small, yellow clods on top. These clods are separated from the butter-milk and put in a bowl where the rest of the water is worked out. It is then salted, molded, and stamped with some pretty little design. After this is done, it is set in the well or the spring to cool for the table. The process has been long, to some extent tedious, but profitable, because insomuch as it has taken time and care and intelligence, by that much does it have a meaning.
>
> Industrialism gives an electric refrigerator, bottled milk, and dairy butter. It takes a few minutes to remove it from the ice to the table, while the agrarian process has taken several hours and is spread over two or three days. Industrialism saves time, but what is to be done with this time? The milkmaid can't go to the movies, read the signboards, and go play bridge all the time. In the moderate circumstances of this family, deprived of her place in the home economy, she will be exiled to the town to clerk all day. (222–23)

All the other tasks on the farm are performed in the same way—slow, time-consuming, but every time slightly different, always furnishing enough variation to be interesting. At eleven the dinner bell rings and the men come to the house. The mules are watered, put in the stalls, and fed before the men go in for their noon meal, which always has a great deal of form:

> It is, in the first place, unhurried. Diners accustomed to the mad, bolting pace of cafeterias will grow nervous at the slow performance of a country table. To be late is a very grave matter, since it is not served until everybody is present. But only some accident, or unusual occurrence, will detain any member of the family, for dinner is

a social event of the first importance. The family are together with
their experiences of the morning to relate; and merriment rises up
from the hot, steaming vegetables, all set about the table, small hills
around the mountains of meat at the ends, a heaping plate of fried
chicken, a turkey, a plate of guineas, or a one-year ham, spiced, and
if company is there, baked in wine. A plate of bread is at each end of
the table; a bowl of chitterlings has been set at the father's elbow; and
pigs' feet for those that like them. (225–26)

Lytle insists that each dish "has a peculiar meaning" to
the consumer for "everyone has had something to do
with the long and intricate process from the consumer
to the table." He does not look upon the product of his
personal labor at "so many cents a pound, or his corn at
so much a dozen" (227).

After the day's work is done and the evening meal
completed, the family gathers in the parents' bedroom,
and one of the boys begins to play the guitar and sing a
traditional ballad. Boys from the neighborhood drop in
to court. After the crops are laid by, such gatherings are
likely to turn into play-parties, where games are played
and songs sung that were brought over from the Old
Country and altered to suit the new locale. Sometimes,
too, there are social occasions in which a large part of
the community participates: ice cream socials, all-day
singings with dinner on the grounds, political picnics,
barbecues, and square dances.

Lytle concludes this intentionally idealized picture of
the life of the yeoman farmer with the statement that
the South "should dread industrialism like a pizen
snake," for the pioneering phase of Southern culture
has long since passed (234). The Southern farmer must
not allow his section to become a materially acquisitive
society; he must not think of the product of his labor in
terms of its material value. Lytle then gives a warning of
what will happen to the family- and land-centered life

that is so complete and satisfying if the farmer tries to turn his farm into a place to make money.

First he will trade his mules for a tractor and pay the difference in cash. Soon the tractor has to be replaced and, since the farmer does not have the available cash to purchase a new one, he buys it on the installment plan. With the tractor he will not need the labor of his sons and they will go into town seeking employment at some service station selling gasoline. Then the farmer buys equipment for the tractor and a truck. These additions—and a Delco engine to pump the water, furnish power for lighting the house and barn, churning the milk, and operating a refrigerator—require him to mortgage his land. Since there is nothing for the girls to do, they go into town seeking employment or hoping to find a husband; therefore the family unit is dissolved. The wife becomes restive because her role has been drastically changed; rather than an essential part of a formal structure, she has become an assistant to a machine. The farmer no longer grows a garden or provides his own meat, and in order to make payments to the bank or to the machinery dealer he sells his cows. His life is moving closer and closer to relying completely on a financial economy. He tries to control nature and finds he cannot. He can plant his money crop, but he cannot make it rain or beat off the hail; neither can he stop the rain when his crop is getting more water than it needs or the soil is too wet for him to cultivate what he has planted. The insects and pests, despite his use of expensive insecticides, are still with him. Since he cannot control the variables of nature, his income is uncertain, but his need for cash is not. The bank, the feed and seed store, the fertilizer company, and the equipment dealer must have their money because they have stockholders and boards of directors to whom they are responsible. When he can no longer meet his payment schedule, he loses his farm. All he can do is to move to town with the hope that he can join his sons at the service station, and, if he cannot, become another of the growing number of unemployed.

The independent, self-respecting farmer must not let this happen to him, his family, and his community. He must, Lytle insists, return to his looms, his handcrafts, his reproducing stock. "Throw out the radio and take down the fiddle from the wall. Forsake the movies for the play-parties and the square dances" (244). The heritage of the self-sufficient farmer, firmly anchored to a specific body of land, surrounded by his family, and immersed in his native culture, is that he is his own man. He must retain his traditional virtues, his self-sufficiency, and his personal integrity.

In "The Life and Death of Cousin Lucius," a biographical sketch based on an uncle of his, John Donald Wade uses another form of argumentation. In Cousin Lucius we see a moving example of a man whose life is lived according to the principles discussed and developed in the other essays. Lucius is an independent, self-reliant man whose life is firmly attached to one specific place about which he has definite feelings, and these feelings propagate an entire cluster of allied actions. He in fact represents Tate's "traditional man." It is almost impossible to determine where his vocation ends and his avocation begins, for he never seems to be quite earning his living and never seems to be free of attempting to.[11] Although he does not ignore the economic forms, he is not unaware of the aesthetic. He is a concrete representation of the Agrarian principle that the test of any society is the kind of men it produces.

Lucius was a boy of fifteen when the Civil War ended, and one of his few memories of that conflict is the day the body of his Cousin Edwin was brought home. He learned from the war and from the death of his mother in childbirth that things are not always dependable, for many of those whom he admired and some of that which he cherished were around in 1861 but they soon passed. He was closely attached to his father who was "honest and kind and capable" and learned to respect the Methodist church, which, his father said, "stimulated" his virtues and aided him in controlling "a certain native irascibleness" (271).

Lucius went away to a small Methodist college where he studied Vergil and Horace, and with his fellow students, though not in the classroom, read the more current writers such as Cervantes, Shakespeare, and Byron. After getting his degree he returned home, and although times were hard he was able to support himself by taking over the local academy. Soon he married, had children, and became a valued and respected man in the community by organizing a debating and literary society and a lending library. His father gave him two hundred and fifty acres of land, and he became a farmer as well as a teacher. "An instinct for the mastery of land," Wade writes, "was in his blood, and he knew few pleasures keener than that of roaming over his place, in the afternoons, when school was out, exulting in the brave world and shouting to his dogs that followed him" (277).

With the coming of a one-crop economy, times changed. The literary and debating society and the library were abandoned, the people saying they had neither the time nor the money to support them. When he began to hear *city* used as an adjective with the inference that anything not *city* was bad, Lucius had to reaffirm his sense of values by turning to history and fable, "telling himself that man had immemorially drawn his best strength from the earth that mothered him, that the farmer, indeed until quite recently, in the South, had been the acknowledged lord; the city man most often a tradesman. . . . He knew little of the philosophy of industrialism, but he knew some people who had grown up to assume that it was the normal order of the world, and he knew that those people left him without comfort" (282–83).

The section shifted from cotton to peaches, became more prosperous and progressive, and demanded that the academy become a public school and teach vocational and technical skills rather than the classics. Although Lucius did not approve of the idea and lost his teaching job, he became president of the local bank. In this position he served well for a time, although he often thought the pace was too fast for him. People would not read anymore; their leisure activities were almost as frenzied as their work. They began agitating for a factory with a huge payroll, and when he advised them to proceed cautiously he was called "an old fogy" and there was talk of removing him from the bank. But he went his way unperturbed because he knew what the young people wanted. They "wanted, without effort, things that have immemorially come as the result of effort only." Lucius waited patiently because, he believed, "The true gods might be long in reasserting themselves, but life is long enough to wait," and he could never get it into his old-fashioned head that "anything less than a complete integrity will serve as a right basis for anything that is intended to mount high and to keep high." He tried to convince his fellow citizens that "the expansion

of his community be an ordered response to actual demands," not a reaction to false desires created by advertising and salesmanship (292).

He was cautious and thrifty and with his extra cash
bought more land. When prosperity returned and the
price of land rose, rather than "an old fogy" he was
called "a wise old bird," for he could see the folly of an
agricultural community trying to live like an industrial
one. He lived to see the land stripped of its trees and the
people abandoning their farms for the city. He continued securely and serenely happy, immersed in his
traditional heritage, until one fine morning he died in
his fields giving his cry of exultation as a covey of quail
flew past him. In his conclusion Wade for the first time
overtly gives his unconcealed approval of the manner of
man this agrarian society has produced: "And all who
wish to think that he lived insignificantly and that the
sum of what he was is negligible, are welcome to think
so. And may God have mercy on their souls" (301).

Some of the essays not surveyed here present other
means of defending "the life and values of the traditional Southern community in the face of the forces of
change that were bent upon transforming it." H. C.
Nixon's "Whither Southern Economy?" and Frank
Owsley's "The Irrepressible Conflict" are persuasive examples of the use of statistical analysis. In "Education,
Past and Present" John Gould Fletcher insists that the
purpose of education is "to teach us to make good use of
what we are" (93). Then he proceeds to demonstrate,
mostly by unsupported statement, not evidence, that the
classical and humanistic education of the Old South was
vastly superior to the scientific and technical training of

1930. In a similar manner Stark Young, like a seer or prophet from on high, proclaims the dire consequences of our abandoning the manners, the *noblesse oblige*, and paternalistic feeling of personal obligation to those less fortunate than we—attitudes that were the very essence of antebellum culture. Henry Blue Kline's "William Remington: A Study in Individualism," like Wade's gracefully written essay, details the means by which a man of breeding is imbued with the traditional virtues.

As we look for an explanation of the continued popularity of a book which is purportedly economic in intent but which presents only a very few definite and feasible economic proposals, it might be helpful to look more closely at exactly what it hoped to accomplish. To my knowledge no other book of its kind in twentieth-century literature offers as many different kinds of argument in defense of a single principle: to delineate what is essential as opposed to what is superficial and destructive in human society. The purpose of my discussion of the different kinds of rhetorical devices used in *I'll Take My Stand* is not to argue that this wide variety is the result of deliberate choice. Instead I am suggesting that given their wide divergence in training, talent, and perspective—and the book's rather haphazard process of composition—the contributors to *I'll Take My Stand* achieved a remarkable coherence of vision.

THREE

Prophets All

ALMOST ALL OF THE AGRARIANS JOINED THE MOVEMENT
for different reasons. Donald Davidson was convinced
that what he was being asked to accept in the name of
progress was vastly inferior to that which he was expected to give up. He never surrendered, he wrote later,
"to the servile notion that the existence of a powerful
'trend' is a mark of its 'inevitability.' All the works of men
result from human choices, human decisions. There is
nothing inevitable about them." He did not believe in
1930, and he was even less convinced when he died
nearly forty years later, "that industrialism can provide
a cure for social and economic ills."[1] Allen Tate, who
never suspected the movement could be effective "in
any immediate political program," submitted his essay
with the hope that it would indicate to some readers the
compelling need for a return to religious humanism.[2] At
a reunion of the Fugitives in 1956, Robert Penn Warren
indicated that the Agrarian movement attracted him because of his concern for the "disintegration of the notion of the individual in the society we're living in." The
result of such a process, he said, is that "you have no individual sense of responsibility and no awareness that
the individual has a past and a place."[3]

John Crowe Ransom insisted that a mature society
must nurture both its economic and its aesthetic forms.
If the economic forms are "short routes to success," the
means by which we gather the material necessities of

life, the aesthetic forms are essential to civilized living. No great society, he said, has ever existed without a poetry, and he insisted that we should not expect ours to be an exception. He was, in short, calling for a society in which poetry was written and read.[4] By the time his *Poems and Essays* appeared in 1955 he was very skeptical that poetry could ever again be an important social form. In the complex modern society, one could hardly expect the work of any artist to have a profound effect on a broad segment of its population. Instead he argued that each artist has his readers, his followers, and they form a community of letters. It is only when we bring these various "communities" together that we have a force to be reckoned with. "How could a gentle civilization," he asks, "do without this community? The oversensitive among us would be solitary and miserable, full of guilt and fears, in our dark privacy, if there were not the generous imagination of the artist to release us."[5] Although he changed his mind considerably regarding the role of the artist in society, he never deemphasized his importance.

I'll Take My Stand remains today, as Richard M. Weaver referred to it almost thirty years ago, "one of the few effective challenges to a monolithic culture of unredeemed materialism."[6] But it is obvious that the place of the black man in the social order provided the contributors to *I'll Take My Stand* with a dilemma they could not satisfactorily solve in 1930. (Warren's *Integration* and *Who Speaks for the Negro?* address this question many years later.) As significant as that dilemma was and remains (in implementation at least) even today, it is hardly fair to say, with F. Garvin Davenport, Jr., that the pervasiveness of this problem vitiated the efforts of the Agrarians to deal effectively with the evils inherent in "the decision of society to invest its economic resources in the applied sciences."[7] Neither can we dismiss the symposium with Virginia Rock's rather arch disclaimer that its primary importance is as a means of studying "Utopian-Conservatism." The Agrarians did not hope, as she suggests, to destroy the realities of a mechanistic materialism.[8] Louis Rubin is much nearer the mark in his statement that *I'll Take My Stand* "makes no real economic proposals for dispensing with what the machine age can offer; it hardly even defines what agrarianism is, other than something generally involving a society in which farming is of importance; it says a great deal about what is wrong with industrialism, but almost nothing about how to get rid of it."[9]

Actually the place of the black man is only one of the many practical programs which the book does not attempt to solve; it also says nothing about the Federal Land Bank, absentee landlords, or sharecropping. Although Lytle and others do mention somewhat casually the unhappy results of applying the principles of industrialism to agriculture, none of them, surely, could foresee the evils of "agribusiness" described by Wendell Berry in *The Unsettling of America*. From an article in *National Geographic* Berry quotes a description of a fully automated farm:

"Attached to a modernistic farm house, a bubble-topped control tower hums with a computer, weather reports, a farm-price ticker tape. A remote-controlled tiller-combine glides across a 10-mile long wheat field on tracks that keep the heavy machine from compacting the soil. Threshed grain, funneled into a pneumatic tube beside the field, flows into storage elevators rising close to a distant city. The same machine that cuts the grain [simultaneously] prepares the land for another crop. A similar device waters neighboring strips of soybeans as a jet-powered helicopter sprays insecticides.

"Across a service road, conical mills blend feed for beef cattle, fattening in multilevel pens that conserve ground space. Tubes carry the feed to be mechanically distributed. A central elevator transports

the cattle up and down, while a tubular side drain flushes wastes to
be broken down for fertilizer. Beside the farther pen, a processing
plant packs beef into cylinders for shipment to market by helicopter
and monorail. Illuminated plastic domes provide controlled en-
vironments for growing high-value crops such as strawberries, toma-
toes, and celery." [10]

To complete his picture, Berry quotes from a project
prepared by agricultural engineering students at the
University of South Dakota:

"Livestock will be housed . . . in a 15-story . . . building. . . . At
capacity, the high-rise building will house 2,500 feeder cattle, 600
cow-calf units, 500 dairy cattle, 2,500 sheep, 6,750 finishing hogs,
space for 150 hogs and litters, 1,000 turkeys, and 15,000 chickens.

"Crops will be grown year around under plastic covers that provide precise climate control. . . . At any given time, regardless of
weather, one field or crop will be in the planting stage, another in the
growing stage, and the third in the harvesting stage.
. . . .
"If tillage is needed, it will be done by electromagnetic waves." [11]

In both farms, one man in a bubble-top tower operates the whole farm by remote control. Through the use
of computers, radio and radar, atomic power (to provide power for the machines, level mountains, and open
irrigation ditches for the plastic-covered fields), man
has conquered his most dangerous adversary; he has
learned to control nature. Needless to say, this is not the
kind of farm Lytle or any of the other Agrarians had in
mind; instead it is a nightmarish vision of what can happen when a society decides "to invest its resources in the
applied sciences." Although it is doubtful that even the
most active imagination among the Agrarians could
have realized the horrors that current technology has
made possible, all of them would readily perceive the
effect of such a system on the human being:

[People] will not live where they work or work where they live. They
will not work where they play. And they will not, above all, play

where they work. There will be no singing in those fields. There will be no crews of workers or neighbors laughing and joking, telling stories, or competing at tests of speed or strength or skill. There will be no holiday walks or picnics in those fields because, in the first place, the fields will be ugly, all graces of nature having been ruled out, and, in the second place, they will be dangerous.[12]

Undoubtedly this is the kind of thing Ransom was referring to when he said that a people who commit themselves to a doctrine of progress initiate "an infinite series" and live without aim, goal, or purpose; that to set up such an establishment is to "assume that labor is an evil, that only the end of labor . . . is good." To believe that nature is used solely for its rewards is "to brutalize man," destroy his sensibilities, and render him unable either to appreciate the arts or to maintain such amenities as manners, customs, rites, rituals, and ceremonies. Finally the effect of such utilitarianism is to dehumanize man by destroying his right relationship to nature, to his fellow man, and to ultimate reality.

I hope you will forgive my trying to establish my point by giving briefly two illustrations from my own experience. I live in a suburb nine miles from Nashville. Having occupied our house for about ten years, my family has the distinction of having the second longest tenure in the neighborhood. Our next-door neighbor, a home builder, has occupied his house about three months longer than we have ours; for the most part, however, the houses—about a dozen or so on a dead-end street— are occupied by young executives for national corporations. One of my neighbors told me a couple of years ago that he had moved eighteen times in twenty years of marriage, but that he had *settled in* in Nashville—had joined a country club, a church, a civic club; his wife was active in school-sponsored events and was a leader in the League of Women Voters. His children loved the school they attended. His daughter was elected homecoming queen and his son was quarterback on the football team. Just as he and his family were assuming a responsible position in the community, however, he received a letter from the New York office of his employer congratulating him on his achievements during his thirty months in Nashville, giving him a promotion that carried with it a handsome increase in salary, and informing him that the firm thought he had earned a position carrying increased responsibilities. The letter asked if he would prefer the position of general manager of the territory supervised by the Dallas office or that under the Washington-Baltimore office. Neither of these suggestions really pleased him; he liked Nashville and wanted to stay there, even though he knew he would have to sacrifice the salary increase and the impressive title; furthermore, he understood, he would seriously jeopardize his chances for further promotions. But he liked his home, his community, and was convinced he could live comfortably on what he earned and have time for some of the things—fishing, camping, travel—he had always wanted to do before the children grew up; and they were almost grown and would soon leave for college. When he found that his family agreed with him enthusiastically and unanimously, he wrote his superior, thanking him sincerely but suggesting that he and his family liked living where they were. After serious consideration, therefore, he had decided to decline the promotion. The answer to his letter came in a telephone call from a local motel. It was from a vice-president of the corporation who had come down from New York, inviting my neighbor to have dinner with him. Over cocktails, steak and lobster, the vice-president carefully explained to my friend that he had misunderstood the content of the original letter. He was not being given the option of Dallas, Washington, or Nashville. His choice was Dallas, Washington, or resignation, because, as the vice-president meticulously explained, "We have followed your career carefully and we think you have the qualities necessary for top-level management. We want you eventually to come to the home office in New York. That's why we have attempted to familiarize you as completely as possible with our entire operation. But we cannot have a man in a senior management position in the company who is not absolutely loyal." "In other words," my friend told me soon after his return from this meeting, "the center of my thoughts and affections must be the company. My feeling toward it must not be mitigated by love of family, friends, or community. I wonder why I was always told to take an active part in community activities wherever I was. Because it was good for business?" Then, after a while he murmured, as he prepared to leave, "They may *think* they own me body and soul."

Last year I visited this family in their new $200,000 house in a Virginia village about an hour outside of Washington. Well, I thought, after a pleasant dinner and a joyful reunion, all he had to sacrifice was community loyalty, a feeling of being *someone* belonging *somewhere*, a sense of family unity, the opportunity to enjoy the aesthetic pleasures of life, and any possible conviction that his individual preferences could control his future. But the family laughed a lot and seemed to take great pleasure in showing me their giant TV screen (it covered half a wall in the den), the new MG sportscar they had just purchased for their son, and the Winnebago in which they were going to tour the West the following summer, if the husband could just get a few days off and if the energy crunch would ease off a little. I wondered if Donald Davidson would have said, "So be it!"

My next example is even more personal. Many years ago, when I first came to Nashville, at the end of each month I took my salary check down to the bank and deposited it. More often than not I knew the teller who handled the transaction and we would exchange greetings and a few inconsequential remarks as he—or she— prepared my receipt. Then there came the day when I went in to cash a check and the person behind the counter did not know me; in order to confirm that my account had sufficient funds to cover the amount of the check, she had to dial an office downtown. Some clerk there checked the account to see if there were sufficient funds in it. Finally there came a time when the computing equipment was sophisticated enough so that when the teller called the downtown number the computer would read my balance, put it on tape, and the tape would give the balance in my account—all of this in a few seconds. The older method required two or three minutes.

Now I no longer deposit my salary check. I am given an employee's number and on the first of each month our computer at the University notifies the one at the bank how much to deposit in my account. If at any time during the month I need to cash a check or transact any other business with the bank, except negotiate a loan for more than two thousand dollars, I drive up to an "Anytime Teller," a booth with no one in it. If I have several small checks to deposit in my account, I press the appropriate button, and the form I need appears. I list the checks, total them, enter my account number on the form, and place it all in a slot marked "Deposits." If all the information I have given is correct, a computerized voice tape from the empty booth says, "Thank you, Mr. Young," and I drive away. If the information I have given is not correct, my form is rejected and another printed message says, "I'm sorry, Mr. Young, but you have made an error in addition." I add the figures again, reinsert the form and the same voice says, "I'm sorry, Mr. Young, but you *still* have an error in addition." And so it continues until I hear "Thank you, Mr. Young." It matters not that our public schools, by common agreement, are less effective than they have been in fifty years; that our unemployment rate is higher than it has been since the depression; or that our economy is bound to a system of planned obsolescence and an internal combustion engine for which we cannot get the fuel to operate. We do have an almost completely automated banking system, and we have demonstrated that the society that decides "to invest its economic resources in the applied sciences" can achieve some unbelievably spectacular results.

 2

The significance of *I'll Take My Stand* is its cry of outrage at the attempts of man to deify the machine, at the amount of time and energy devoted to emphasizing the inevitability of a technocratic society, and at the concerted attacks on man's basic humanity. Above all, it is a passionate protest against the creation of an intellectual climate in which the Hellenistic-Hebraic values cannot exist. The Agrarians stood firm against the modern form of gnosticism which insists that through the proper application of scientific achievements the social planners can effect a perfect world inhabited by perfect human beings. The Agrarians argued repeatedly that modern man has lost his sense of vocation, his attachment to place, his conviction that he is an individualized human being performing a valuable function or service in a specific, concrete place.

One of the book's basic values to present-day readers

is, in the words of Professor William Pratt, its insistence that "a satisfying way of life cannot be produced by economic forces, with their shifting cycles of poverty and wealth, but can only come from an adherence to stable human values and ideals." Increasing technology threatens the quality of human existence, Pratt says. "The unchecked exploitation of nature can become suicidally destructive; when the very air we breathe, the food we eat, and the water we drink have become poisoned by rampant urbanism and industrialism, and we are running rapidly out of fuel for our machines, all Americans—not merely Southerners—can draw moral, spiritual, and aesthetic refreshment from the essays in *I'll Take My Stand*."[13]

Louis Rubin argues that *I'll Take My Stand* is not of the literary genre of "works such as *The Republic, Das Kapital*, or the *Nouvelle Héloïse*, with their proposals and systematic master plans for the reorganization of society along Utopian lines." Rather, he says, "it is [in] the tradition of Cooper's *The American Democrat*, Thoreau's *Walden* and, the American Scholar Address—works that censured the abuses of the age."[14] Lewis P. Simpson sees *I'll Take My Stand* as implicitly "a literary evocation of what may be called the 'pastoral moment,' . . . the moment when the human consciousness became aware of its own existence—the moment when it responded to a differentiation between existence as essentially ahistorical (as cosmic, cyclical, a compacted unity) and existence as historical (as linear and endlessly changing)."[15] Such moments, Simpson concludes, may be found in Western literature in the works of Theocritus, Vergil, Sidney, and Shakespeare.

I'll Take My Stand also evokes the moment in American literature when Emerson, exasperated at the direction in which America's daring new experiment in democracy had turned, exclaimed: "Things are in the saddle and are riding men!" A few years later Henry David Thoreau, in complete agreement with his older friend and mentor, decided:

> The mass of men lead lives of quiet desperation. What is called resignation is confirmed desperation. From the desperate city you go into the desperate country, and have to console yourself with the bravery of minks and muskrats. A stereotyped but unconscious despair is concealed even under what are called the games and amusements of mankind. There is no play in them, for this comes after work.[16]

Thoreau determined to go to Walden Pond, not "to live cheaply nor to live dearly there, but to transact some private business with the fewest obstacles." He tells us a little later what his business was and why Walden Pond was a good place to transact it:

> I went to the woods because I wished to live deliberately, to front only the essential facts of life, and see if I could not learn what it had to teach, and not, when I came to die, discover that I had not lived. I did not wish to live what was not life, living is so dear; nor did I wish to practise resignation, unless it was quite necessary. I wanted to live deep and suck out all the marrow of life, to live so sturdily and Spartan-like as to put to rout all that was not life, to cut a broad swath and shave close, to drive life into a corner, and reduce it to its lowest terms, and, if it proved to be mean, why then to get the whole and genuine meanness of it, and publish its meanness to the world; or if it were sublime, to know it by experience, and be able to give a true account of it in my next excursion.

He left the woods, he said, because he had "several more lives to live, and could not spare any more time for that one." Presumably he thought that he had learned from this experience what he could; therefore he should move on to others. Those of us who have studied Thoreau's masterpiece know this Yankee philosopher learned many things during his stay at Walden. His suspicion was confirmed: the meaningless clutter of urban centers tends to corrupt man and place needless obstacles in his way as he attempts to lead the good life. In writing of his experiences at Walden, Thoreau reduced his actual time there from two years, two months, and two days to one year in order to demonstrate that human life can be lived in tune with the natural cycle, the seasonal change from summer to autumn, winter, and spring. As in nature, he observed in himself the deterioration of old matter and the development of new. When he left Walden amid the burgeoning of spring, he was conscious of new life within him, a spiritual rebirth, so that he was able to proclaim the goodness of life properly lived, "to brag as lustily as chanticleer in the morning, standing on his roost, if only to wake my neighbors up."

We are all aware, of course, of the hazards inherent in attempting to compare Emerson and Thoreau with the Agrarians. There are surely as many differences between the men from Concord and those associated with Nashville as there are similarities. Few, if any, of the Nashville group believed in man's natural goodness, or in his perfectibility, not to mention his divinity. All of the Agrarians perhaps—and surely Ransom, Tate, Davidson, and Warren—would have disagreed with Emerson's proclamation that as Jesus was divine so are we all; the only difference between Jesus and the average citizen of Concord was that the man from Nazareth had the "temerity to proclaim his divinity to the world." Neither would they have been completely in accord with Emerson's doctrine of self-reliance or Thoreau's notion that "If a man does not keep pace with his companions, perhaps it is because he hears a different drummer." Instead the Agrarians insisted on the necessity of one's assuming his natural role in society. From social forms come social order and only in an ordered society—one that fosters and nurtures aesthetic forms (rites, rituals, ceremony, manners, religion)—can civilization exist. The flawed antebellum society that Tate presents in *The Fathers*, a social order tainted with slavery but one that operated under the restrictions of a highly developed social code, is described by Lacy Buchan, the narrator and protagonist, as follows: "Our lives were eternally balanced upon a pedestal below which lay an abyss I could not name." Tate is suggesting that any society effected by man bears the imperfections of its creators, and these imperfections can be held in abeyance only by what Ransom calls the aesthetic forms. Only a strict adherence to a fixed, severely demanding social code keeps Lacy, his family, and friends from being destroyed by falling headlong into the abyss, by succumbing to the strong, unceasing, destructive demands of their natural and irrational urges.

The Southerners were naturally suspicious, therefore, of transcendental inner voices, the unaided visions that would supersede tradition and mythopoetic document as a means of knowing ultimate reality. They did agree with their New England predecessors, however, in insisting that the good life is the examined life, that man should attempt to establish a right relationship with nature. Although they did not share Thoreau's belief that the ownership of property was an unnecessary encumbrance, they would surely have agreed that nature regarded solely as a commodity is an oversimplified and false conception of nature. Like Emerson and Thoreau, the Agrarians insisted that if one is to live in society at the highest level which his consciousness permits, he cannot drift aimlessly and allow social and political matters to develop as they will. He must think actively and act consciously in order to shape the kind of society in which he can live as a complete human being. There is another point of agreement. Thoreau wrote: "Actually the laboring man has not leisure for a true integrity day by day; he cannot afford the manliest relations to man." In the introduction to *I'll Take My Stand*, Ransom observed that in modern society labor is assumed to be an evil; "only the end of labor or the material product is good." Therefore, labor is brutalizing; it is no longer "one of the happy functions of human life" and man has lost his "sense of vocation" (xl–xli).

Both *Walden* and *I'll Take My Stand* employ homely but highly figurative prose, and the battle cry in both books is the same. Man's natural rights include his access to the human function of living which an unnecessarily complicated technocratic society tends to destroy. Unless the Southerner reacts now to simplify his life, as Thoreau told his contemporaries a hundred and fifty years ago, he is doomed, in the words of Andrew Lytle, "to hop about like sodium on water, burning up in his own energy" (202). He must make a truce with nature, not live in constant war against it. As Thoreau says:

> Let us spend one day as deliberately as Nature, and not be thrown off the track by every nutshell and mosquito's wing that falls on the rails. . . . If the engine whistles, let it whistle until it is hoarse for its pains. If the bell rings, why should we run. Let us settle ourselves and work and wedge our feet downward through the mud and slush of opinion, and prejudice . . . that alluvium which covers the globe through Paris and London, through New York and Boston and Concord . . . till we come to a hard bottom and rocks in place, which we can call *reality*.

Nearly thirty years after the publication of *I'll Take My Stand*, Donald Davidson declared that he and his comrades were engaged in a desperate search for reality:

> We wanted to get away from mere expedients and get down—or up—to first principles. We were saying that life should determine economics, and not economics life. Our quarrel was not with indus-

try or science in their proper role, but with industrialism as a tyrant enslaving and ruling science itself, and with it religion, the arts, education, the state, thus reducing all principles to one principle, the economic, and becoming a destroyer, ready to break the continuity of human history and threatening the very existence of human society.[17]

Thoreau's main argument, as I have said, was for human freedom; the Agrarians were pleading for the continuation of the "community of human history," for the perpetuation of human society. Thoreau was convinced that adherence to the demands of organized society often dulled the sound of the inner voice telling man what he must do. The Agrarians insisted, on the other hand, that man could move from barbarism to civilization because his natural impulses were controlled and directed by the rules and orders of organized society. Only by following the rites, rituals, codes, and ceremonies of a traditional society is man able to avoid falling into the abyss. Though the theological perspectives of Thoreau and the Agrarians were at odds, the means by which they attempted to accomplish their social and political objectives were often identical.

 3

As Douglas Knight has pointed out, "As a tract in economics, *Walden* . . . is absurd." Thoreau's account of his sojourn at Walden Pond is intended to prepare the reader for two truths, that (1) "A man is rich in proportion to the number of things which he can afford to let alone," and (2) "The cost of a thing is the amount of what I will call life which is required to be exchanged for it, immediately or in the long run."[18] Because the intentions of his masterpiece were misunderstood, Thoreau's reputation was for nearly a century in almost total eclipse. He was called a "skulker," a man who, unable or unwilling to meet the demands and challenges of modern social living, escaped to the wilds of nature where he lived on beans, beets, and huckleberries. Some of Thoreau's critics, such as James Russell Lowell and Robert Louis Stevenson, missed the principal burden of his argument. Thoreau was not insisting that "complicated civilization" was altogether absurd. It is true, as Lowell observes, that he "squatted on another man's land; he borrowed an ax; his boards, his nails, his bricks, his mortar, his books, his plow, his hoe." [19]

Thoreau, I think, would be the first to agree that without these material things, products of an advanced and fairly complicated society, his time at Walden would have been duller and much less profitable. The last thing he is suggesting is that man should sever completely his ties with society and live in absolute seclusion, at Walden Pond or anywhere else, for years at a time. He does encourage every man, however, to find his Walden Pond and to live there as long as he needs to, leaving behind everything he can afford to do without. As Rubin notes, Thoreau's basic intention, it would seem, is to urge his contemporaries to reexamine their assumptions concerning the minimum necessities for the good life.

His own close observation of nature was proposed, not as a universal model to be followed, but as a way of showing how the possibilities of consciousness were being glossed over or obscured by the slavish, unexamined bondage to material possessions, by men who "through mere ignorance and mistake, are so occupied with the factitious cares and superfluously coarse labors of life, that its finer fruits cannot be plucked by them." To point out impracticalities or inconsistencies in Thoreau's specific arrangements at Walden Pond . . . is irrelevant. [20]

To dismiss the central intent of the Agrarians because they did not deal adequately with the plight of the black man in the South, as F. Garvin Davenport has done, is to denigrate Thoreau for his apparent lack of compassion regarding the immigrant Irish railroad builders—thence ignoring the central thrust of *Walden*: to awaken his neighbors to the dangers of sacrificing, in Ransom's term, the aesthetic values for the economic ones demanded by a materially acquisitive society. America did not heed his warning and quickly the great American experiment in democratic government deteriorated into the domain of the Robber Barons. Such an emphasis, Henry James decided, could only result in a cultural desert; he escaped to the more hospitable intellectual climate of Europe. Similarly, after returning from a visit to America, Matthew Arnold commented that he found the civilization in the new world culturally arid and unexciting.

As Thoreau's warning that American social forms were emphasizing too many of the wrong values went unheeded, so has that of the Agrarians. For seventy-five years or more Thoreau was accused of being a social hermit, of wanting to reverse the tide of progress and revert to a more primitive stage of human existence. In a similar manner the Agrarians for almost fifty years were accused of being idealistic college professors and men of letters afraid to attempt to cope with the complexities of the twentieth century, of trying to turn back the clock a hundred years so that they could live in the peace and contentment of the paternalistic society of the 1830s. Being members of the ruling class, they would be insulated from—or could philosophize away—the brutalizing, dehumanizing, barbaric system of human slavery. Time after time in the years after its appearance, *I'll*

Take My Stand was ridiculed and condemned, its authors called ivy-tower romantics and neo-Confederates. Only within the past few years, when the quality of life has deteriorated to the point that it is difficult to find clean air to breathe or pure water to drink, when we realize that the fuel necessary to operate the combustion engines of our industrial state is being rapidly exhausted, when our standard of living has dropped from first place to ninth in the world, when the American dollar is no longer the strongest currency in the world, when we realize that an increasing number of nations (and perhaps a few individuals who have clipped articles from the popular press) have the means of destroying all human life—only after all of these developments, I say, have we come to read, really read, a book that proclaims that a civilization which emphasizes "economic values" to the detriment of "aesthetic values" does so at its own peril.

"Our vast industrial machine . . . ," Ransom warns in his essay in *I'll Take My Stand*, "is like a Prussianized state which is organized strictly for war and can never consent to peace" (8). "The artist," Davidson points out, "is no longer *with* society . . . he is *against* or *away* from society" (43). A society that invests almost all of its resources in the applied sciences under the guise of progress, of improving the nature of the world and that of those who inhabit it, is one that thrusts its citizens on a treadmill, always in search of the perfection that has eluded them and always will. Few books in the literature of America confront the problems that have eternally plagued its citizens—problems that are elusive and paradoxical to the point of insolubility—in a manner so provocative and compelling as *I'll Take My Stand*.

FOUR

Postlude

ACTIVITIES OF THE AGRARIANS IN SUPPORT OF THEIR cause did not cease with the publication of *I'll Take My Stand*, nor did the debates offered in defense of its principles. As the grip of the Great Depression tightened on the economic system, several of the Agrarians attempted to convince the general public that their philosophical recommendations could be used as an effective means of meeting the challenges to the economic well-being of the entire country through the formation of the Southern Policy Committee. Virginius Dabney was elected chairman and Davidson served on the committee. In a meeting held in Atlanta, April 25–28, 1935, and chaired by H. C. Nixon, two objectives were adopted: (1) "To extend throughout the South the organization of local Public Policy Committees. . . ." and (2) "to encourage consideration . . . of questions which directly affect the interest of the [local] community; State; the South; and the Nation."[1]

Since they had begun to plan their symposium, several members of the group had considered other means of disseminating their attitudes and convictions—including the acquisition of a county newspaper, a magazine, and a press. In the spring of 1933 Seward Collins wrote Davidson, who was spending a year of academic leave in Marshallville, Georgia, with his old friend John Donald Wade, that he was thinking of establishing a

journal, the *American Review*, to publish four groups of
writers: the Humanists, the Neo-Thomists, the Agrarians, and the Distributists.[2] In his response Davidson
persuaded Collins to come to Nashville to discuss the
possibilities of such a journal with as many of the Agrarians as he could get together. Collins came, and the talks
went so well there that after a time the group retired to
Cornsilk, the Lytle family plantation near Guntersville,
Alabama. There a general agreement was reached, and
for the first time the Agrarians had a journal of national
circulation in which they could offer their pronouncements.

They were not at all backward in seizing this opportunity to circulate their ideas. The first three issues of
the *American Review* carried contributions by Davidson,
Fletcher, Lytle, Owsley, Ransom, Tate, and Warren.
During the next four and a half years, the lifetime of the
magazine, the Agrarians published more than sixty essays in its pages (Davidson, twenty; Ransom, eleven;
Fletcher, eight; Lytle, three; Owsley, six; Tate, six;
Wade, one; Warren, seven). Every Agrarian except four
—Young, Kline, Lanier, and Nixon—contributed at
least one essay. Another journal that welcomed materials from the Agrarians, as well as the Southern New
Critics, was the *Southern Review*, founded at Louisiana
State University in 1935, with Robert Penn Warren and
Cleanth Brooks as managing editors. During the seven
years of its existence this distinguished publication carried essays and reviews by almost all of the major contributors to *I'll Take My Stand*.

In the spring of 1936 the Agrarians and Distributists held a meeting to discuss a more broadly based
convention. A proposed conference at Northwestern
University the next year was not successful because
some members of the group, especially Allen Tate, were

given neither honoraria nor expenses for attending. Davidson, Ransom, and Herbert Agar, who at the time was working with Tate on the second Agrarian symposium, *Who Owns America?*, did participate in discussions of "the problems and possibilities of social distribution and an integral life in the modern world."[3]

The primary difference between the essays that appeared in such journals as the *American Review* and the *Southern Review* in the period between the two symposia and those published in *I'll Take My Stand* is that these later articles tend to be more practical and less theoretical than the earlier ones. Some of them, such as Owsley's "The Pillars of Agrarianism" and Nixon's "Social Security for the Farmer" offered definite solutions to specific problems. Nixon's *Forty Acres and Steel Mules* stated its intention in its introduction: to suggest "a broader program of agricultural reconstruction than I read into the writings which have come from most members of the Agrarian group since 1930."[4] Even Ransom's "Happy Farmers," which he contributed to the *American Review* in 1935, differed markedly in tone from his essay in *I'll Take My Stand.* Although he was still calling for men who "are economic dualists," he was no longer primarily concerned with the theoretical issues of Progress and Service and their destructive effects upon the principles of American democracy; now he was convinced that our "broad acres" not only should be the "feed-bowl of the Western world" but that they should also furnish a home and a livelihood for farmers "with more room, and more heart, than most of the farmers of the world, happy farmers." Ransom's cast of mind and his rather idiosyncratic prose style did not permit him to write simple straightforward solutions to practical economic problems such as those found in the writings of Owsley and Nixon, but he was trying.

Almost since the appearance of *I'll Take My Stand,* furthermore, many of the contributors to that collection were talking about a second symposium. Davidson wrote Tate on October 29, 1932, suggesting the kind of book he thought it shoud be: "The book should make full use of the present trends toward the farm and small towns; of regionalism in *art* and *economics*" [italics mine]; there is no doubt that Davidson wanted this symposium to address itself to more practical issues than the first one had. At almost the same time Andrew Lytle reported that he had been working with Lyle Lanier on a detailed plan of how "five million people" could be returned to the land. In order that their second book offer material assistance in bringing this plan into being, it "should deal with the basic matters of . . . the farms and the farmers themselves."[5] About the time Ransom and Davidson began actively to seek a publisher for a book offering a more practical defense of Agrarian principles, they discovered that the University of North Carolina Press was going to publish W. T. Couch's *Culture in the South,* to which Davidson, Wade, Lytle, and Nixon had been asked to contribute essays. (Lytle's essay was rejected.) Ransom insisted that Tate review the book since at least half of its contributors had mentioned *I'll Take My Stand,* although not all of the comments were favorable.

Tate's review appeared in the *American Review* for February 1934. In spite of Ransom's admonition that his remarks be "wise, fixed and not repelling," Tate's attitude toward the book is revealed in his statement that none of the contributors to *I'll Take My Stand* was allowed to discuss economic issues (Davidson wrote on literature, Nixon on higher education, and Wade on humor). To Tate the book was obviously a liberal document intended to answer some of the Agrarian arguments offered in *I'll Take My Stand*. Quoting from Couch's preface that he did not consider, as the Agrarians apparently did, "that farming in the South is a healthy and attractive occupation, peculiarly devoted to the services of genuinely human purposes," Tate moves to comment on the contribution of Broadus Mitchell:

> I have tried for years to understand what is wrong with Mr. Mitchell. There being, he says, no Old Southern culture that he "can see," it would be well to get more factories in the South. Industrialism is not only the superior economic structure for society; it is also "determined" economically. It is beautiful to observe the forces of history at the service of Mr. Mitchell's desires; I envy him. . . . Although labour troubles in the South have been grievous, they have not been grievous enough. We must catch up with the world; we must completely industrialize the South so that we shall have a problem that must be solved in socialist terms. There is a moral imperative upon us to do this. This point of view, I gather from certain intimations *passim* in Mr. Mitchell's essay, is "realistic"; that of the Agrarians, backward-looking and sentimental.[6]

From this fairly representative comment, Tate's view of *Culture in the South* is unmistakable. Like Tate, no reader of this book could consider it an adequate sequel to *I'll Take My Stand*, despite the fact that three of the contributors to the Agrarian symposium were represented in it.

Although Tate indicated that he hoped for a closer relationship between the Nashville Agrarians and the North Carolina group, the two were irreconcilably opposed at fundamental points and the hoped-for rapprochement never occurred. By the winter of 1933 a sequel to *I'll Take My Stand* was underway, but as it developed, this book was to be drastically different from its predecessor. After Tate had read Herbert Agar's *The People's Choice*, he invited Agar, who at the time was serving as London correspondent for the Louisville *Courier-Journal*, to write for the *American Review*. Agar's essays in that journal convinced Tate, about a year later, to be-

come co-editor of *Who Owns America? A New Declaration
of Independence* (1936). Although eight Agrarians (Tate,
Lytle, Davidson, Ransom, Wade, Nixon, Owsley, and
Warren) as well as some more recent converts (Cleanth
Brooks, George Marion O'Donnell, and James Waller)
published essays in it, this volume is far different from
its predecessor.

In the first place, as Davidson later pointed out, the
book was carefully planned by the editors, and the kind
of "group consultation" that had been such an important part of the foundation of *I'll Take My Stand* was
entirely missing. Too, points of view other than the
Agrarians' were represented, particularly those of the
Anglo-Catholics and the Distributists, so the appearance
of dedication to a single cause was conspicuously absent.
Most important, the contributions of the four major
Fugitive-Agrarians were noticeably weaker when considered as separate parts of one clearly defined argument. Ransom's contribution, "What Does the South
Want?", which had previously appeared in the *Virginia
Quarterly Review,* not only is generally inferior to his
"Reconstructed but Unregenerate," but it seems to reveal Ransom's declining interest in the cause. Tate's
"Notes on Liberty" is as opaque as his "Remarks on the
Southern Religion," but it seems to lack the ring of sin-
cerity and the urgency for specific action that character-
ize the earlier essay. Warren's "Literature as a Symp-
tom," although among his most distinguished critical
writings, clearly underscores the peripheral nature of
his interest in Agrarianism. Among the four, only Davidson's "That This Nation May Endure" demonstrates
that his interest in the specific principles of Agrarianism
is undiminished. Not only are the basic tenets of the essay clearly and cogently argued, but it presages Davidson's upcoming *The Attack on Leviathan: Regionalism and*

Nationalism in the United States (1938), the most persuasive argument in American literature for retaining sectional and regional identity. As students of Davidson's
writing know, this premise was at the center of his every
literary endeavor until he died some thirty years later.

On September 7, 1936, soon after *Who Owns America?*
was published, Ransom wrote Tate:

In Sunday's *Banner* you will see my review of *Mediterranean*, if you
think it worth a dime, which it hardly is. Excuse the performance in
view of the medium. However, it has started me on an exciting ex-
cursion of thought which I want to bring before you. I say there in
one place that *patriotism* is eating at lyricism. What is true in part for
you (though a part that is ominously increasing) is true nearly in full
for me: *Patriotism* has nearly eaten me up and I've got to get out of
it.[7]

A few months later he wrote Tate that he was "signing
off" from Agrarianism "but a little by degrees."[8] Not
long after that, when he was considering an offer from
Kenyon College, he could without exaggeration write
his chairman, Professor Edwin Mims, that he could do
the kind of writing he wanted to do as well in Ohio as he
could in Tennessee. "It is true," he wrote on June 8,
1937, "that if [the writing he proposed to do] were on
regionalism or agrarianism, I would be going into for-
eign parts. But I have about contributed all I have to
those movements, and I have of late gone almost entirely into pure literary work."[9] No longer was his primary literary interest centered in joining a group of
friends of similar persuasion in defending a social order
of a specific kind. He was eager to complete a study, now
delayed more than twenty years, of the nature and function of poetic discourse.

A year later, when he was attempting to get the *Kenyon Review* underway, he sent out flyers asking prospective writers for contributions for the journal. Written at

the bottom of the printed invitation mailed to Davidson was a scrawled note: "I do want things from you—poems, critiques, reviews (I'm sorry we won't be in the field for patriotic and agrarian things)—and the sooner the better."[10] Ransom's final declaration of independence from Agrarianism comes in his published reaction to W. P. Southard's "The Religious Poetry of Robert Penn Warren." As long as Southard's remarks are on the literary qualities of Warren's verse, Ransom is in complete accord; but when the essay near the end veers off into social commentary Ransom demurs:

> It seemed that we had taken our constitutional and predestined development, and our progress was irreversible; but suddenly Mr. Southard proposes to found an agrarian community within which innocence may be recovered. I can reproach him for his phantasy with the better conscience inasmuch as I have entertained it too, as one of the Southern agrarians. And it seems to be in order to offer a brief notice about that, though I will not pretend to be representing Mr. Warren, or Mr. Tate, or others of that group.[11]

Before Ransom published the essay he sent a copy to Tate, requesting his opinion of it. Tate urged him "to suppress" it on the ground that "when one finds a new interest, one need not repudiate an old one: one simply moves on."[12] Davidson's reaction to the published essay was one of anger and disappointment. "It is all right for John to change his mind," Davidson wrote Tate on October 3, 1944; "furthermore there have been other occasions when he swung an axe wildly, not much regarding his friends."[13] What Tate and Davidson were not fully aware of, apparently, was that Ransom had put social and economic criticism aside, as he had poetry twenty years before, and had moved back to his first love, literary theorizing. In 1938 he had published his first important essays of literary criticism, *The World's Body*, and three years later the second, *The New Criticism*, appeared. For the remainder of his life most of his creative energy was expended in formulating and developing his theory of the nature and function of poetry.

The year 1936 also was an important date in Tate's movement away from the Agrarian cause. Although he followed the advice he had given Ransom and did not publicly "repudiate the cause," readers of his *The Mediterranean and Other Poems* (1936) can see a different cast to Tate's thought. No longer is he primarily concerned with reestablishing a social order in which religious humanism can be a compelling force in human behavior, he is obviously troubled that man is unaware of the deep schism that has rent asunder the culture of the Western world. There is a vast abyss separating the areas of human thought and behavior controlled by the reason and those dominated by the emotions. This untransversable chasm must be closed, he was convinced, or Western civilization was doomed. We must control our material acquisitiveness, make our "journey Eastward," and recover our spiritual roots if we expect our culture to survive. After 1936 he wrote few essays and poems that can be classified as Agrarian in intent. Instead he published such essays as "Literature as Knowledge," "Tension in Poetry," and "The Symbolic Imagination," and poems like "Seasons of the Soul." Like Ransom, he too was interested in literary criticism, but, unlike his old friend, his work clearly marks the road leading to his conversion to Roman Catholicism.

Although Robert Penn Warren's interest in the deterioration of individual freedom under big government, big business, and a materially acquisitive economic order continued, he wrote few economic and political essays. (A few years later he became conspicuously involved in the race question.) Most of his time and energy were devoted to the creation of poetry and fiction, and to the innovative editing (with Cleanth Brooks) of their influential textbooks. He published *Thirty-Six Poems* in 1935, his first novel *Night Riders* in 1939, *Understanding Poetry* (with Brooks) in 1938, and *Understanding Fiction* (also with Brooks) in 1943. Despite Davidson's continued attempts to make his readers ever mindful of the importance of reconstituting a social order like that of the Old South, Southern Agrarianism as a significant movement in the development of American political and social thought ended about 1936. Although *I'll Take My Stand* retained a few devoted readers over the years, its rediscovery as an important social and philosophic document has been a literary phenomenon of the past two decades.

Notes

Chapter One

1. *Fugitive*, 1 (April 1922), 3.
2. *Southwest Review*, 10 (April 1925), 13–14.
3. *Fugitive*, 4 (December 1925), 125.
4. Thomas Daniel Young, *Gentleman in a Dustcoat: A Biography of John Crowe Ransom* (Baton Rouge: Louisiana State University Press, 1976), p. 188.
5. Louise Cowan, *The Fugitive Group: A Literary History* (Baton Rouge: Louisiana State University Press, 1959), p. 217.
6. Thomas Daniel Young and M. Thomas Inge, *Donald Davidson* (New York: Twayne Publishers, 1971), p. 62.
7. Cowan, *The Fugitive Group*, p. 216.
8. Donald Davidson, *Southern Writers in the Modern World* (Athens: University of Georgia Press, 1958), p. 40.
9. Young, *Gentleman in a Dustcoat*, p. 198.
10. Donald Davidson, "The Artist as Southerner," *Saturday Review of Literature*, 2 (May 15, 1926), 783.
11. Donald Davidson, "First Fruits of Dayton: The Intellectual Evolution in Dixie," *Forum*, 79 (June 1928), 896–907.
12. Twelve Southerners, *I'll Take My Stand: The South and the Agrarian Tradition* (Baton Rouge: Louisiana State University Press, 1977), p. 44.
13. Allen Tate, "*The Fugitive*, 1922–1925: A Personal Recollection Twenty Years After," *Princeton University Library Chronicle*, 3 (April 1942), 84.
14. John Tyree Fain and Thomas Daniel Young, eds., *The Literary Correspondence of Donald Davidson and Allen Tate* (Athens: University of Georgia Press, 1974), pp. 192–98. Hereinafter cited as *Literary Correspondence*.

15. Unpublished letter in the Firestone Library, Princeton University.
16. _Literary Correspondence_, pp. 201–202.
17. Ibid., pp. 221–22.
18. Unpublished letter in the Firestone Library, Princeton University.
19. John Crowe Ransom, "The South Defends Its Heritage," _Harper's Magazine_, 159 (June 1929), 108–18; "The South—Old or New?" _Sewanee Review_, 36 (April 1928), 139–47.
20. Unpublished letter in the Firestone Library, Princeton University.
21. _Literary Correspondence_ p. 227.
22. Ibid., p. 229.
23. Ibid., pp. 230–31.
24. Unpublished letter in the Firestone Library, Princeton University.
25. Quoted in Virginia Rock, "The Making and Meaning of _I'll Take My Stand_: A Study in Utopian-Conservatism," unpublished dissertation, University of Minnesota, 1961, p. 250.
26. The original typescript of this unpublished document is in the Jesse E. Wills Collection in the Vanderbilt University Library.
27. Rock, "The Making and Meaning of _I'll Take My Stand_," p. 228.
28. "Introduction: A Statement of Principles" runs from Page xxxvii to Page xlviii in the edition of _I'll Take My Stand_ published by the Louisiana State University Press. All references are to this edition and page numbers will be given in the text.
29. Young, _Gentleman in a Dustcoat_, pp. 210–11.
30. Unpublished letter in the Firestone Library, Princeton University.
31. Ibid.
32. Personal conversation with the author.
33. Rock, "The Making and Meaning of _I'll Take My Stand_," pp. 252–62.
34. _Literary Correspondence_, p. 255.
35. See Louis D. Rubin, Jr., _The Wary Fugitives: Four Poets and the South_ (Baton Rouge: Louisiana State University Press, 1978), pp. 212–18.
36. Young, _Gentleman in a Dustcoat_, pp. 215–16.

Chapter Two

1. Rubin, *The Wary Fugitives*, p. 237.
2. Cleanth Brooks, in M. Thomas Inge, "The Continuing Relevance of *I'll Take My Stand*," *Mississippi Quarterly*, 33 (Fall 1980), 453.
3. Allen Tate, *Essays of Four Decades* (New York: William Morrow, 1968), p. 583.
4. See Ransom, "The South Defends Its Heritage," pp. 108–18, and "The South—Old or New?", pp. 139–47.
5. John Crowe Ransom, *The World's Body* (New York: Charles Scribner's Sons, 1938), pp. 29–54, reprinted by the Louisiana State University Press, 1968. The page numbers in both editions are the same.
6. Ibid., p. 30.
7. Ibid., p. 31.
8. Ibid., p. 34.
9. Tate, *Essays of Four Decades*, p. 426 ff.
10. Ibid., p. 585.
11. Ibid., p. 556.

Chapter Three

1. Donald Davidson, in "The Agrarians Today: Five Questions," *Shenandoah*, 3 (Summer 1952), 17.
2. Allen Tate, in "The Agrarians Today: Five Questions," p. 28.
3. Rob Roy Purdy, ed., *Fugitives' Reunion: Conversations at Vanderbilt, May 3–5, 1956* (Nashville: Vanderbilt University Press, 1959), p. 209.
4. Ransom, *The World's Body*, pp. 32–38.
5. John Crowe Ransom, *Poems and Essays* (New York: Vintage Books, 1955), p. 117.
6. Richard M. Weaver, "The Tennessee Agrarians," *Shenandoah*, 3 (Summer 1952), 4.
7. F. Garvin Davenport, Jr., *The Myth of Southern History: Historical Consciousness in Twentieth-Century Southern Literature* (Nashville: Vanderbilt University Press, 1970), pp. 79–81. The quotation is from *I'll Take My Stand*, p. xxxix.
8. Rock, "The Making and Meaning of *I'll Take My Stand*," p. 450.
9. Rubin, *The Wary Fugitives*, p. 235.

10. Quoted in Wendell Berry, *The Unsettling of America: Culture and Agriculture* (San Francisco: Sierra Club Books, 1977), p. 67.

11. Ibid., p. 68.

12. Ibid., p. 74.

13. William Pratt, in Inge, "The Continuing Relevance of *I'll Take My Stand*," 455–56.

14. Rubin, *The Wary Fugitives*, p. 237.

15. Lewis P. Simpson, in Inge, "The Continuing Relevance of *I'll Take My Stand*," 458–59.

16. This quotation from Thoreau and the others that follow are from *Walden and Other Writings* (New York: Modern Library, 1950).

17. Davidson, *Southern Writers in the Modern World*, pp. 57–58.

18. Richard Ruland, ed., *Twentieth Century Interpretations of Walden* (Englewood Cliffs, N. J.: Prentice Hall, 1968), p. 11.

19. James Russell Lowell, "Thoreau," in *The Shock of Recognition: The Decline of Literature in the United States Recorded by the Men Who Made It*, Edmund Wilson, ed., 2 vols. (New York: Grosset and Dunlap, 1955), I, 242.

20. Rubin, *The Wary Fugitives*, p. 240.

Chapter Four

1. For detailed discussions of the activities and achievements of this group, see Rock, "The Making and Meaning of *I'll Take My Stand*," pp. 366–68, and Davidson, "Where Are the Laymen? A Study in Policy Making," *American Review*, 9 (October 1957), 456–81.

2. Seward Collins to Davidson, March 8, 1933, Jesse E. Wills Collection, Vanderbilt University Library.

3. Patrick F. Quesin, "Agrarianism and the Jeffersonian Philosophy," *Review of Politics*, 2 (January 1940), 92 fn.

4. *Forty Acres and Steel Mules* (Chapel Hill: University of North Carolina Press, 1938), p. v.

5. Quoted in a letter from Ransom to Tate, February 23, 1933, Firestone Library, Princeton University.

6. "A View of the Whole South," *American Review*, 2 (February 1934), 419–20.

7. Unpublished letter in the Firestone Library, Princeton University.

8. Ransom to Tate, April 6, 1937, unpublished letter in the Firestone Library, Princeton University.

9. Unpublished letter in the Jesse E. Wills Collection, Vanderbilt University Library.

10. Ransom to Davidson, undated, Jesse E. Wills Collection, Vanderbilt University Library.

11. John Crowe Ransom, "Art and the Human Economy," *Kenyon Review*, 7 (Autumn 1945), 686.

12. Allen Tate, "Reflections on the Death of John Crowe Ransom," *Sewanee Review*, 82 (Fall 1974), 550.

13. Unpublished letter in the Firestone Library, Princeton University.

Bibliography

Berry, Wendell. *The Unsettling of America: Culture and Agriculture.* San Francisco: Sierra Club Books, 1977.

Cowan, Louise. *The Fugitive Group: A Literary History.* Baton Rouge: Louisiana State University Press, 1959.

Davenport, F. Garvin, Jr. *The Myth of Southern History: Historical Consciousness in Twentieth-Century Southern Literature.* Nashville: Vanderbilt University Press, 1970.

Davidson, Donald. "The Artist as Southerner," *Saturday Review of Literature,* 2 (May 15, 1926), 781–83.

————. "First Fruits of Dayton: The Intellectual Evolution in Dixie," *Forum,* 79 (June 1928), 896–907.

————. *"I'll Take My Stand*: A History," *American Review,* 5 (Summer 1935), 301–21.

————. *Southern Writers in the Modern World.* Athens: University of Georgia Press, 1958.

Fain, John Tyree, and Thomas Daniel Young, eds. *The Literary Correspondence of Donald Davidson and Allen Tate.* Athens: University of Georgia Press, 1974.

Fifteen Southerners. *Why the South Will Survive.* Athens: University of Georgia Press, 1981.

The Fugitive, April 1922–December 1925. Intro. Donald Davidson. Gloucester, Mass., 1964.

Howard, William C., and Walter Sullivan, eds. *A Band of Prophets.* Baton Rouge: Louisiana State University Press, 1982.

Inge, M. Thomas. "The Continuing Relevance of *I'll Take My Stand,*" *Mississippi Quarterly,* 33 (Fall 1980), 445–60.

Karanikas, Alexander. *Tillers of a Myth: Southern Agrarians as Social and Literary Critics.* Madison: University of Wisconsin Press, 1966.

Purdy, Rob Roy, ed. *Fugitives' Reunion: Conversations at Vanderbilt, May 3–5, 1956.* Nashville: Vanderbilt University Press, 1959.

Ransom, John Crowe. *Poems and Essays.* New York: Vintage Books, 1955.

———. "The South Defends Its Heritage," *Harper's Magazine*, 159 (June 1929), 108–18.

———. "The South—Old or New?" *Sewanee Review*, 36 (April 1928) 139–47.

———. *The World's Body.* Baton Rouge: Louisiana State University Press, 1968.

Rock, Virginia. "The Making and Meaning of *I'll Take My Stand*: A Study in Utopian-Conservatism." Ph.D. dissertation, University of Minnesota, 1961.

Rubin, Louis D., Jr. *The Wary Fugitives: Four Poets and the South.* Baton Rouge: Louisiana State University Press, 1978.

Simpson, Lewis P. *The Dispossessed Garden: Pastoral and History in Southern Literature.* Athens: University of Georgia Press, 1975.

Tate, Allen. *Essays of Four Decades.* New York: William Morrow, 1968.

———. "*The Fugitive*, 1922–1925: A Personal Recollection Twenty Years After," *Princeton University Library Chronicle*, 3 (1942), 75–84.

Thoreau, Henry David. *Walden and Other Writings.* New York: Modern Library, 1950.

Twelve Southerners. *I'll Take My Stand: The South and the Agrarian Tradition.* Baton Rouge: Louisiana State University Press, 1977.

Young, Thomas Daniel. *Gentleman in a Dustcoat: A Biography of John Crowe Ransom.* Baton Rouge: Louisiana State University Press, 1976.

Young, Thomas Daniel and M. Thomas Inge. *Donald Davidson.* New York: Twayne Publishers, 1971.

Index